# HOT FUSS

Music transcriptions by Pete Billmann, Addi Booth and David Stocker

ISBN 0-634-08822-X

**HAL•LEONARD®**
CORPORATION

7777 W. BLUEMOUND RD. P.O. BOX 13819 MILWAUKEE, WI 53213

Visit Hal Leonard Online at
**www.halleonard.com**

# Jenny Was a Friend of Mine

Words and Music by Brandon Flowers, Dave Keuning, Mark Stoermer and Ronnie Vannucci

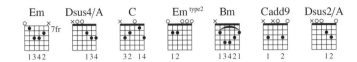

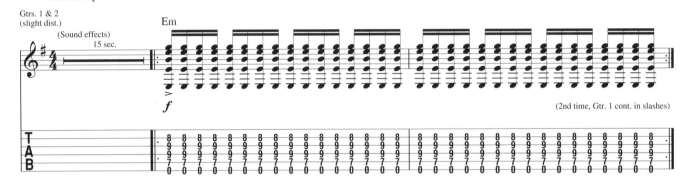

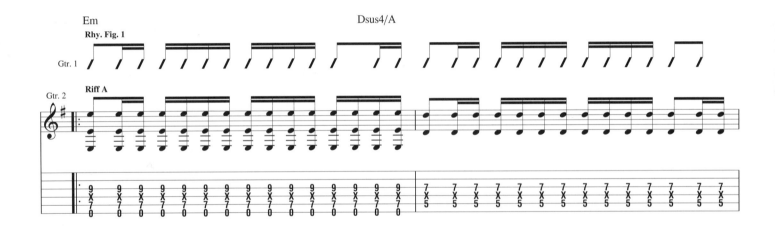

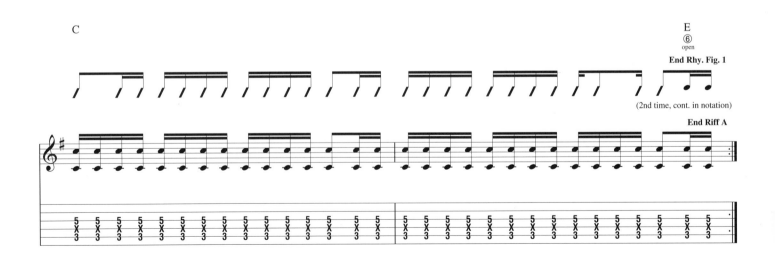

**Verse**

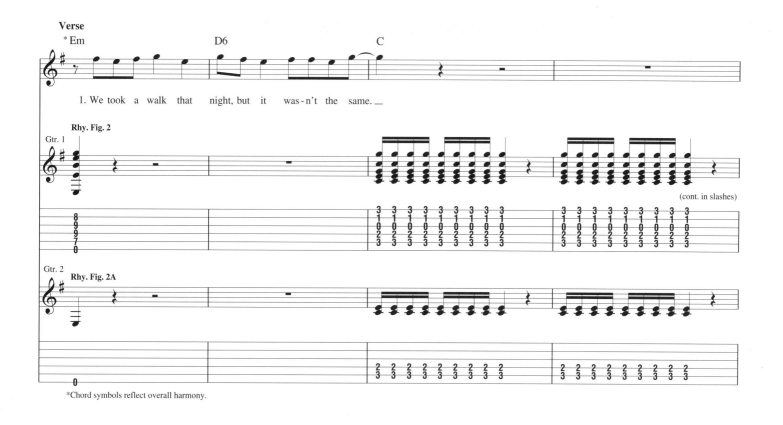

1. We took a walk that night, but it was-n't the same. ___

*Chord symbols reflect overall harmony.

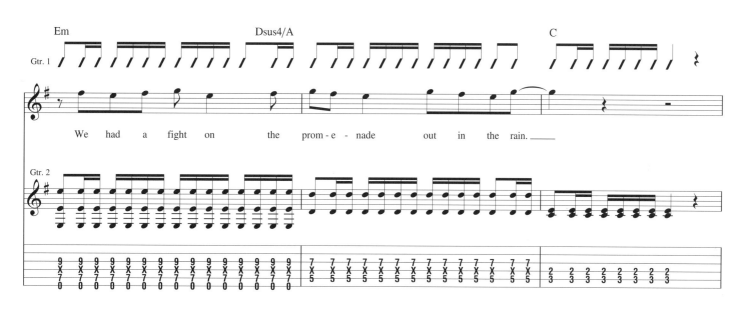

We had a fight on the prom-e-nade out in the rain. ___

Gtr. 1: w/ Rhy. Fig. 1 (2 times)
Gtr. 2: w/ Riff A (2 times)

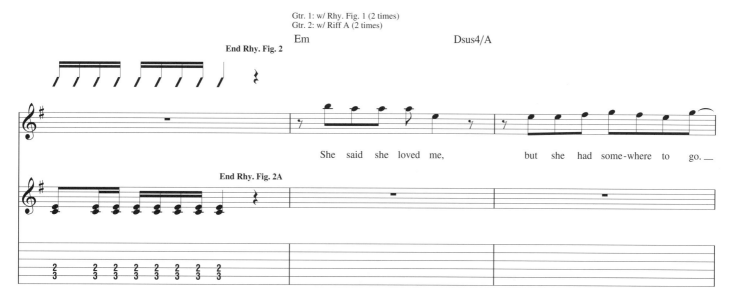

She said she loved me, but she had some-where to go. ___

3

She could - n't scream while I

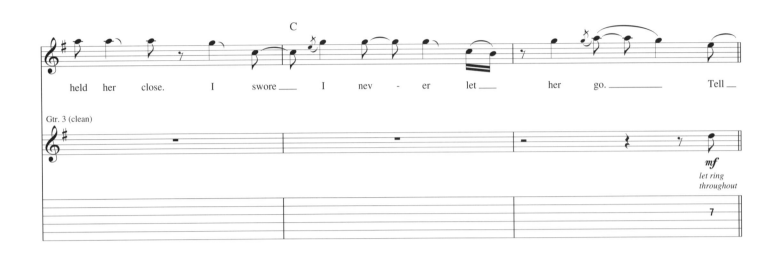

held her close. I swore ___ I nev - er let ___ her go. ___ Tell ___

Gtr. 3 (clean)

*mf*
*let ring throughout*

**Chorus**

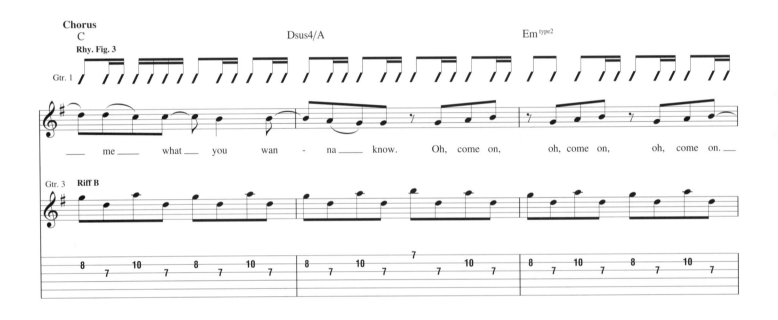

Rhy. Fig. 3
Gtr. 1

___ me ___ what ___ you wan - na ___ know. Oh, come on, oh, come on, oh, come on. ___

Gtr. 3  **Riff B**

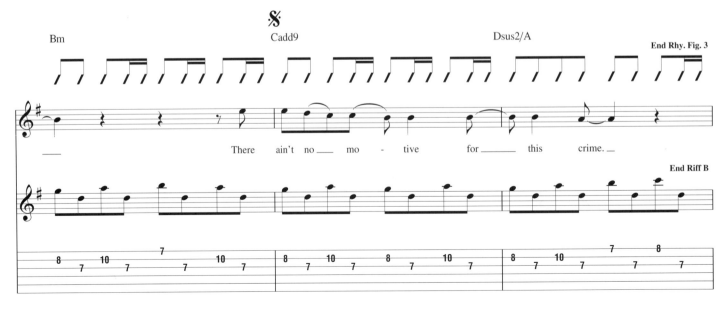

End Rhy. Fig. 3

___ There ain't no ___ mo - tive for ___ this crime. ___

End Riff B

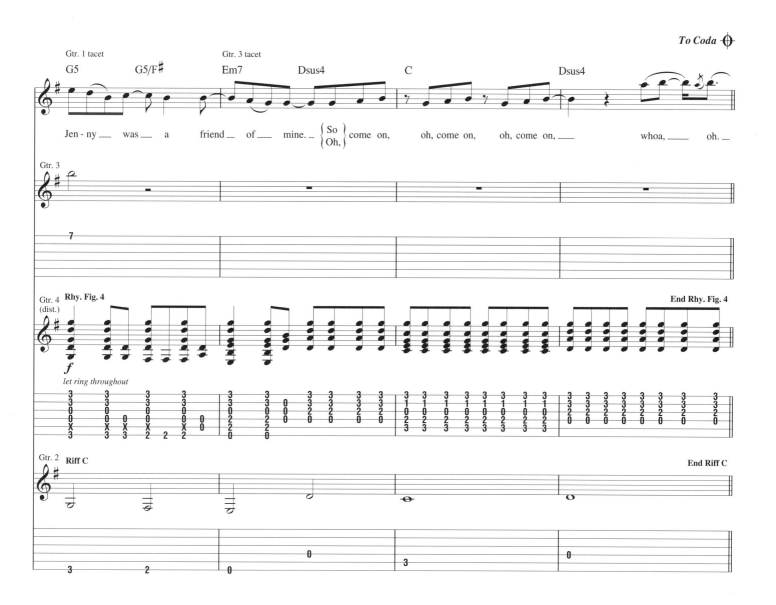

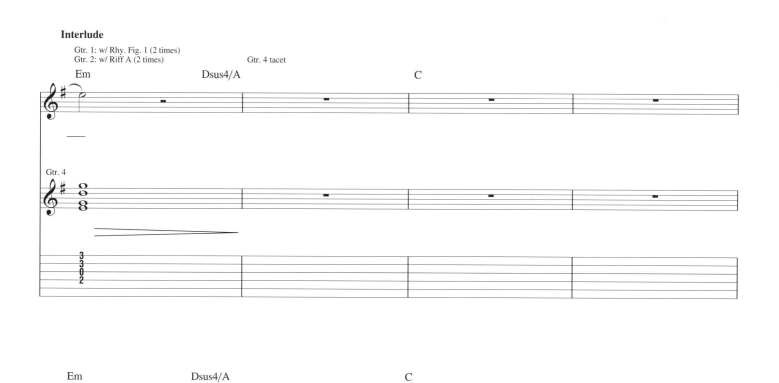

**Verse**

Gtrs. 1 & 2: w/ Rhy. Figs. 2 & 2A

Em                              D6                          C

2. I know my rights. I've ___ been here all day and it's time ___

Em                 Dsus4/A                    C

for me to go, so let me know if it's al - right. ___

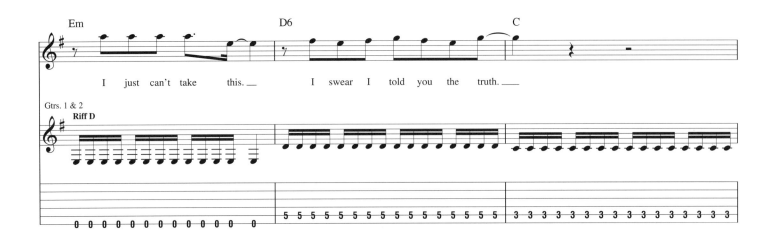

Em                             D6                          C

I just can't take this. ___ I swear I told you the truth. ___

Gtrs. 1 & 2

Riff D

Gtrs. 1 & 2: w/ Riff D

Em                       D6

She could - n't scream while I held her ___ close. I swore ___

End Riff D

**Chorus**

Gtr. 1: w/ Rhy. Fig. 3
Gtr. 3: w/ Riff B

C                                   C                 Dsus4/A

___ I nev - er let her go. ___ Tell ___ me ___ what ___ you wan - na ___ know. Oh, come on,

Gtr. 3

oh, come on,    oh, come on. _____      And then you __ whis - per in ____ my __ ear. __

*D.S. al Coda*

Gtr. 2: w/ Riff C
Gtr. 4: w/ Rhy. Fig. 4

I know __ what __ you're do - in' here.    So come on,    oh, come on,    oh, come on. _____      There

**Keyboard Solo**

Gtr. 1: w/ Rhy. Fig. 5 (3 times)
Gtr. 2: w/ Riff E (3 times)

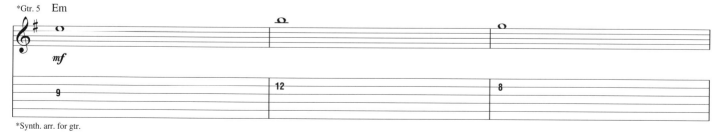

*Synth. arr. for gtr.

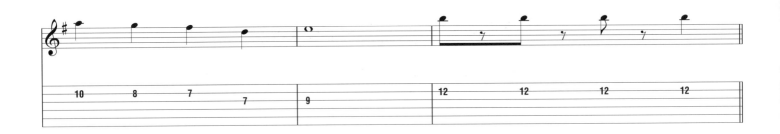

Gtr. 1: w/ Rhy. Fig. 1 (4 times)
Gtr. 2: w/ Riff A (4 times)

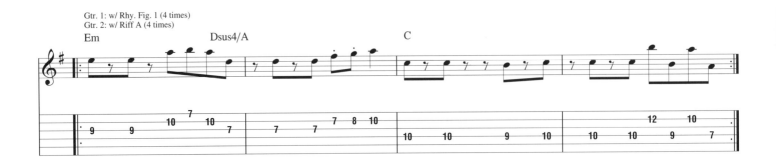

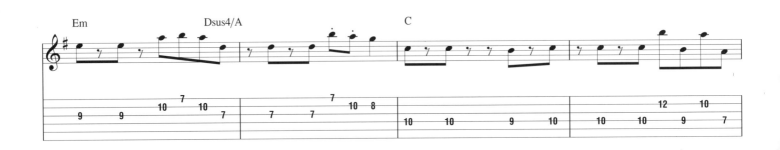

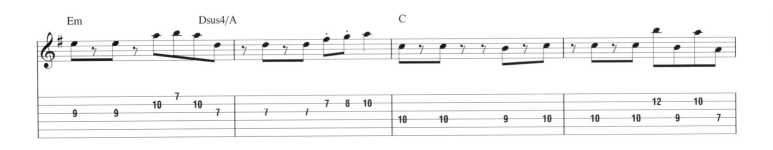

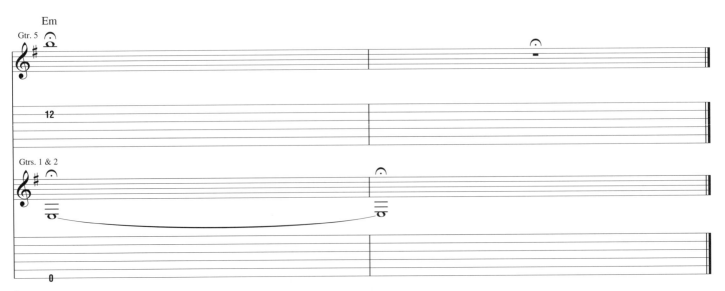

# Mr. Brightside

**Words and Music by Brandon Flowers, Dave Keuning, Mark Stoermer and Ronnie Vannucci**

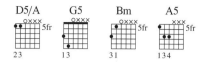

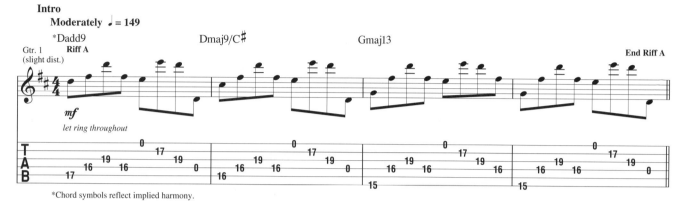

*Chord symbols reflect implied harmony.

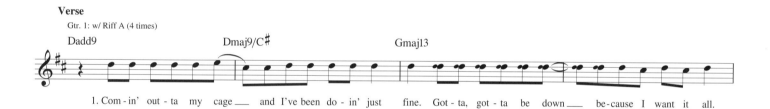

1. Com-in' out-ta my cage ___ and I've been do-in' just fine. Got-ta, got-ta be down ___ be-cause I want it all.

It start-ed out with a kiss. ___ How did it end up like this? It was on-ly a kiss, ___ it was on-ly a kiss. ___

**pp**

fdbk.

*Vol. swell

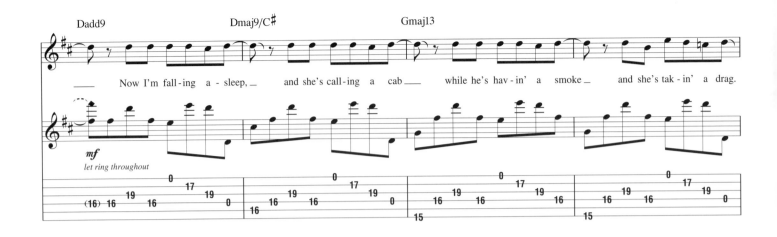

Now I'm fall-ing a - sleep, and she's call-ing a cab while he's hav-in' a smoke and she's tak-in' a drag.

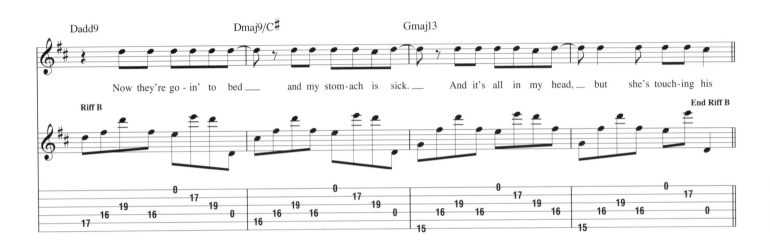

Now they're go - in' to bed and my stom-ach is sick. And it's all in my head, but she's touch-ing his

**Pre-Chorus**
Gtr. 2 tacet

chest. Now he takes off her dress. Now let me

*Composite arrangement

go.

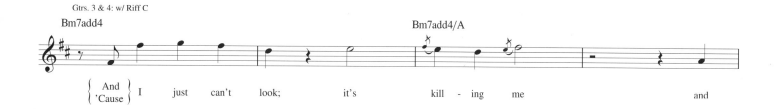

Gtrs. 3 & 4: w/ Riff C

Bm7add4                                        Bm7add4/A

{ And / 'Cause } I just can't look; it's kill - ing me          and

tak - ing ___ con - trol.

Gtrs. 3 & 4

(Gtr. 3, cont. in slashes)

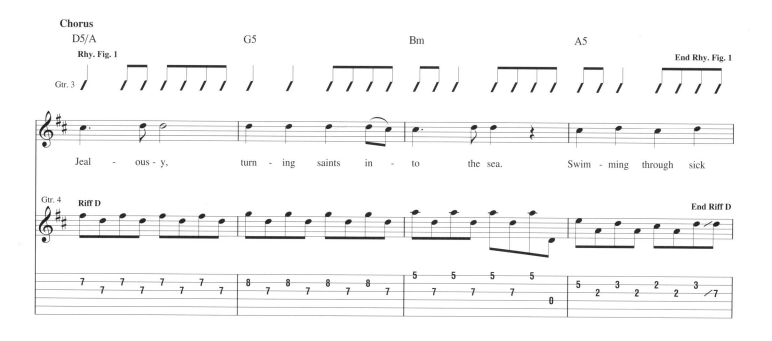

**Chorus**

D5/A                  G5                  Bm                A5

**Rhy. Fig. 1**                                                  **End Rhy. Fig. 1**

Gtr. 3

Jeal - ous - y, turn - ing saints in - to the sea. Swim - ming through sick

Gtr. 4    **Riff D**                                                **End Riff D**

Gtr. 3: w/ Rhy. Fig. 1 (3 times)
Gtr. 4: w/ Riff D

D5/A                  G5                  Bm                A5

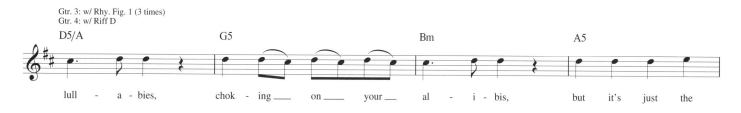

lull - a - bies, chok - ing ___ on ___ your ___ al - i - bis, but it's just the

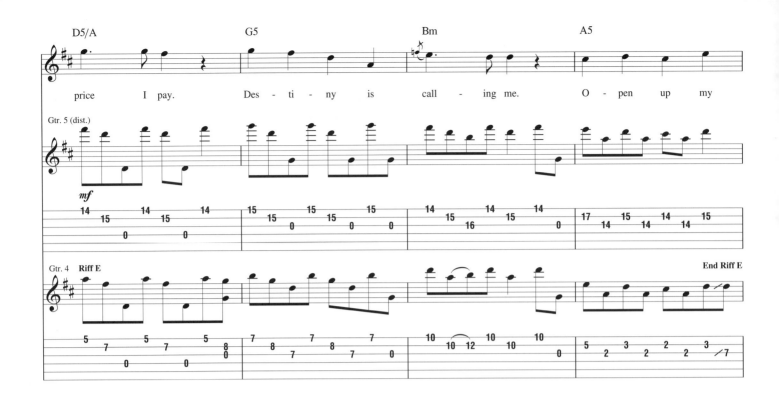

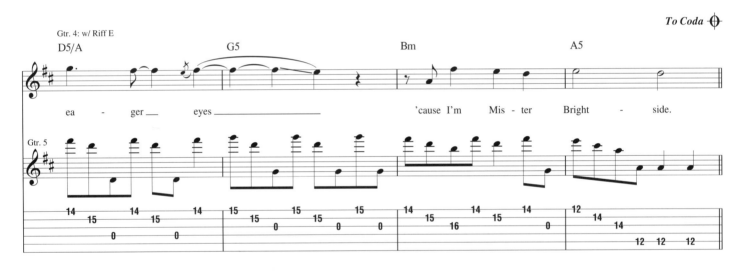

**Interlude**
Gtr. 3: w/ Rhy. Fig. 1 (2 times)
Gtr. 4: w/ Riff D (1 3/4 times)
Gtr. 5 tacet

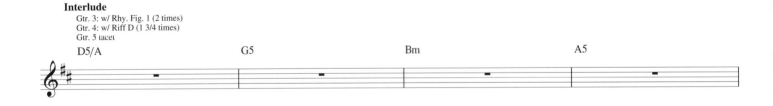

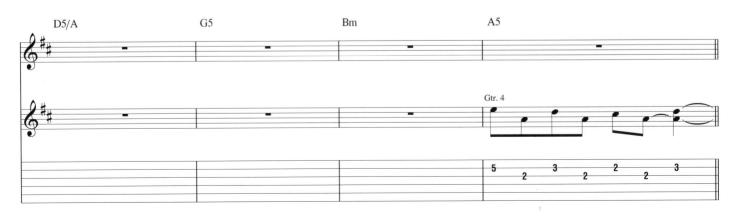

## Verse

Gtr. 1: w/ Riff A (4 times)
Gtr. 2: w/ Riff A (3 times)

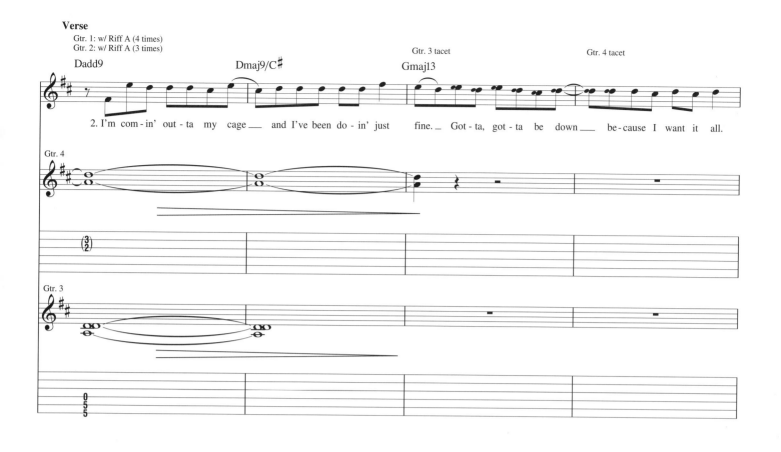

2. I'm com-in' out-ta my cage ___ and I've been do-in' just fine. ___ Got-ta, got-ta be down ___ be-cause I want it all.

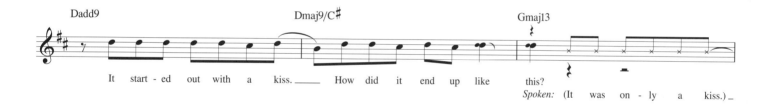

It start-ed out with a kiss. ___ How did it end up like this? ___

*Spoken:* (It was on-ly a kiss.) ___

It was on-ly a kiss. ___ Now I'm fall-ing a-sleep, ___ and she's call-ing a cab ___

___ while he's hav-in' a smoke ___ and she's tak-in' a drag. ___ Now they're go-in' to bed ___

___ and my stom-ach is sick. ___ And it's all in my head, ___ but she's touch-ing his

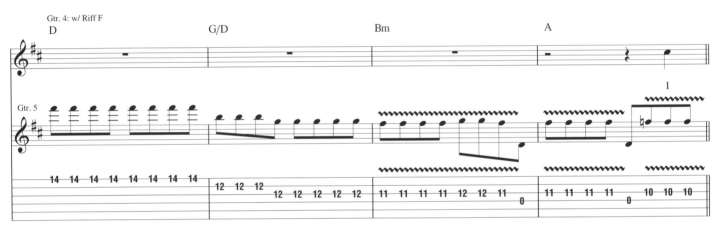

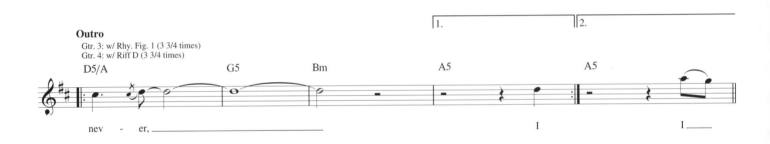

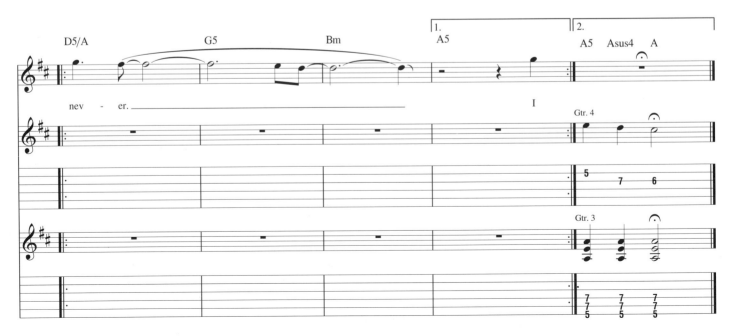

# Smile Like You Mean It

**Words and Music by Brandon Flowers, Dave Keuning, Mark Stoermer and Ronnie Vannucci**

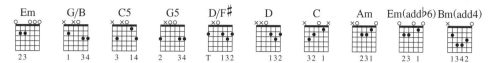

Tune down 1/2 step:
(low to high) E♭-A♭-D♭-G♭-B♭-E♭

**Intro**
**Moderately** ♩ = 125

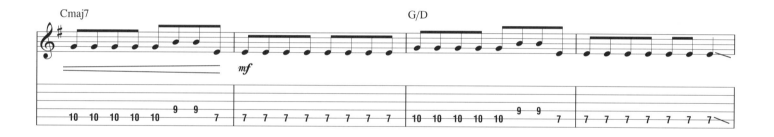

*Fade in      **Chord symbols reflect overall harmony.

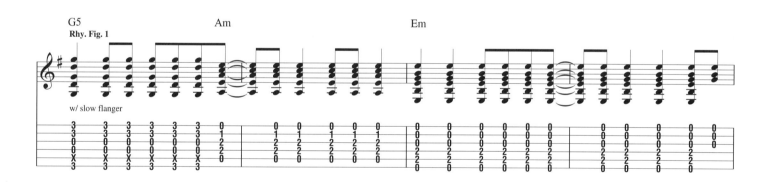

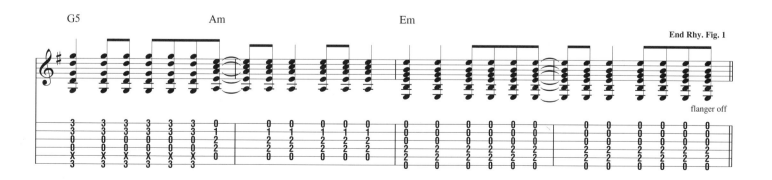

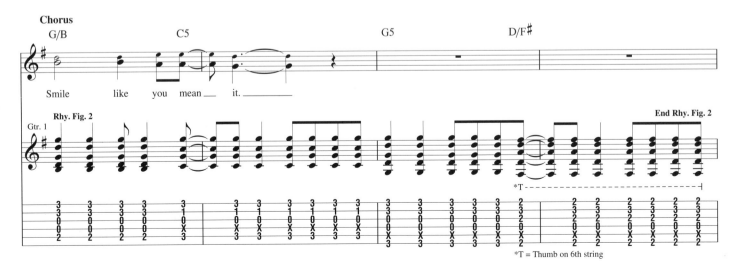

Smile like you mean ___ it. ___

**Verse**

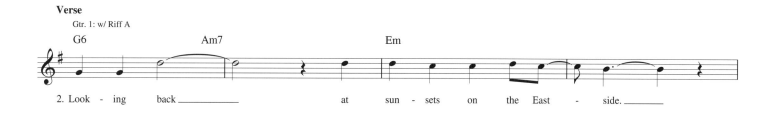

2. Look-ing back ___ at sun-sets on the East-side. ___

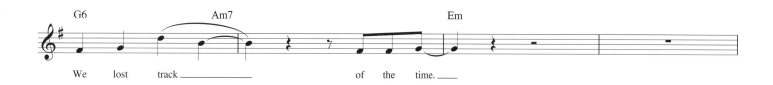

We lost track ___ of the time. ___

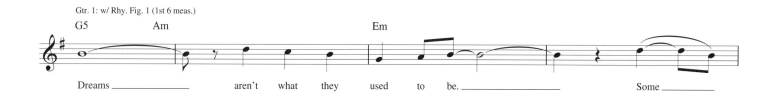

Dreams ___ aren't what they used to be. ___ Some ___

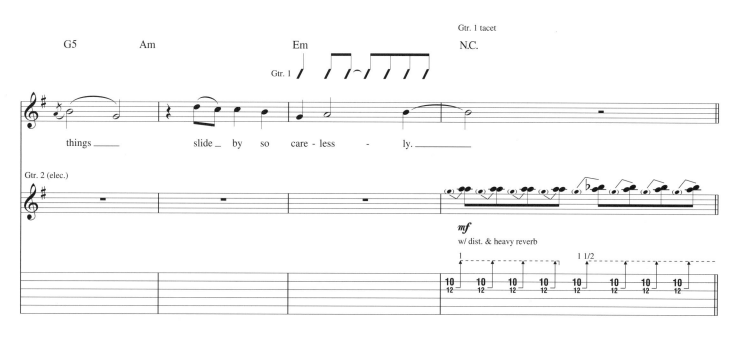

things ___ slide by so care-less - ly. ___

**Chorus**

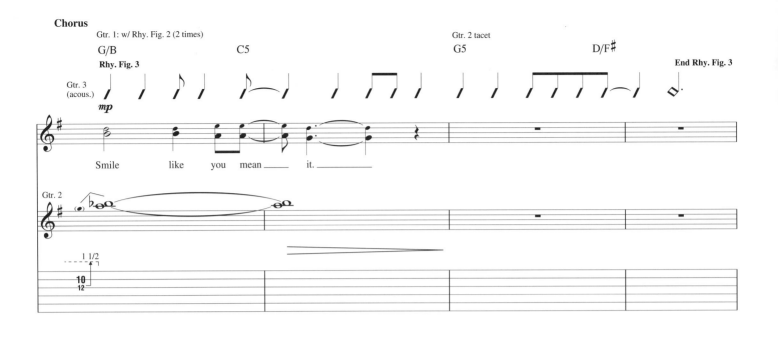

Smile like you mean it.

Smile like you mean it.

**Guitar Solo**

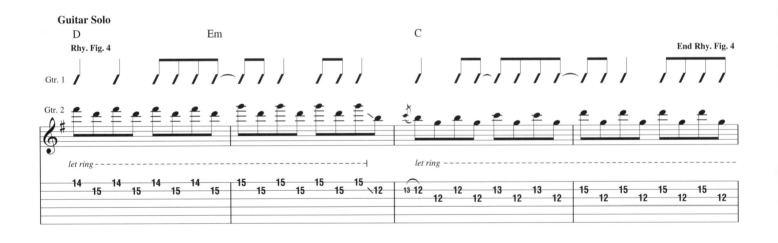

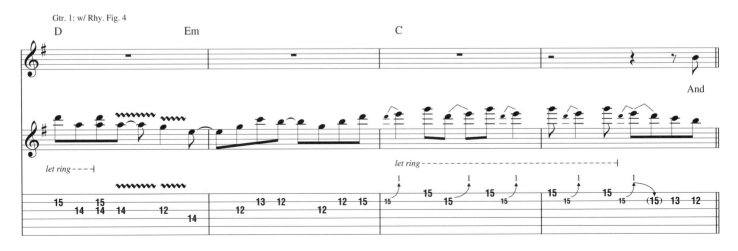

And

**Interlude**

*w/ digital vocal harmonizer & flanger

Gtr. 1: w/ Rhy. Fig. 5
Gtr. 2: w/ Riff B

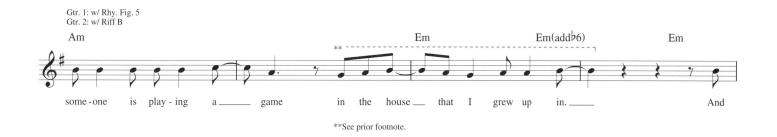

**See prior footnote.

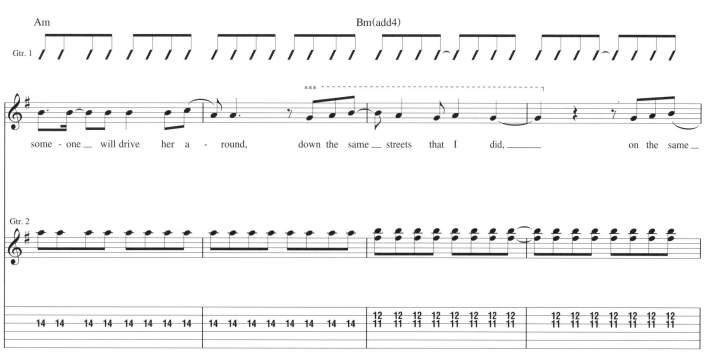

***See prior footnote.

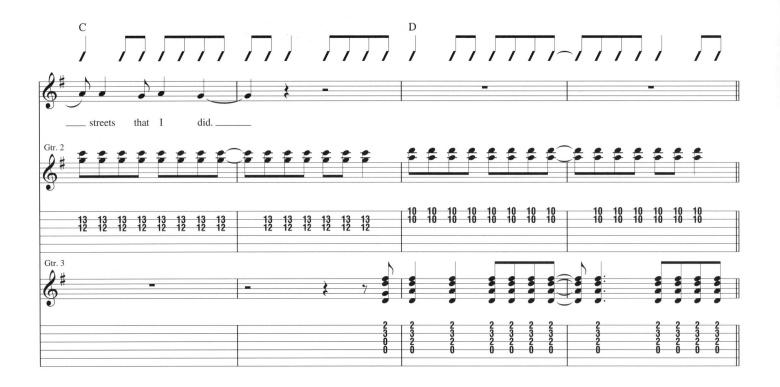

streets that I did.

Gtr. 2

Gtr. 3

## Chorus

Gtr. 1: w/ Rhy. Fig. 2 (4 times)
Gtr. 2 tacet
Gtr. 3: w/ Rhy. Fig. 3 (4 times)

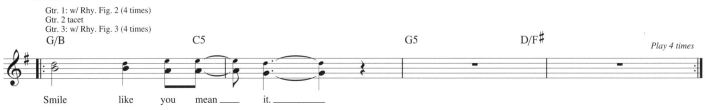

Smile like you mean it.

## Outro

Gtr. 1: w/ Rhy. Fig. 1 (1st 4 meas.) (2 times)

Oh, no, oh, no, no, no.

*2nd time, w/ echo set for quarter-note regeneration
w/ 16 repeats (fade out).

Gtr. 1

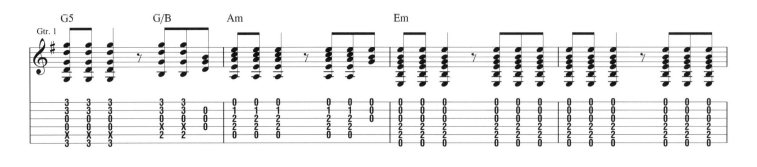

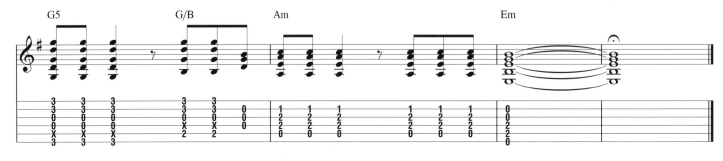

# Somebody Told Me

**Words and Music by Brandon Flowers, Dave Keuning, Mark Stoermer and Ronnie Vannucci**

Tune down 1/2 step:
(low to high) E♭-A♭-D♭-G♭-B♭-E♭

**Intro**
**Moderately** ♩ = 138

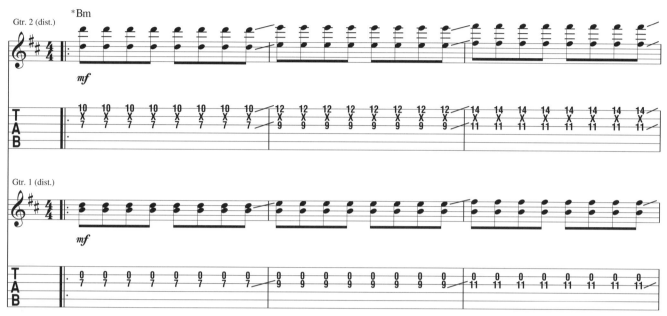

*Chord symbols reflect overall harmony.

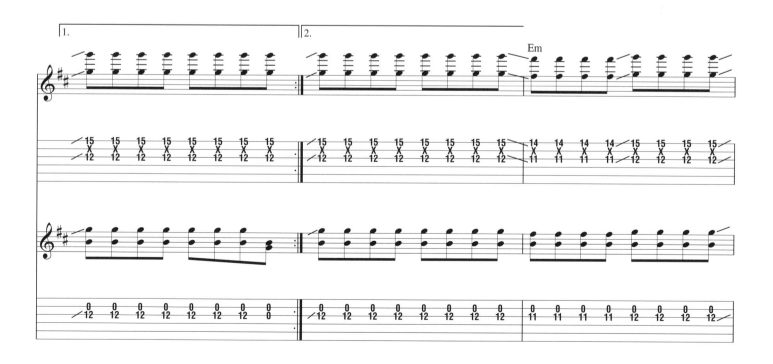

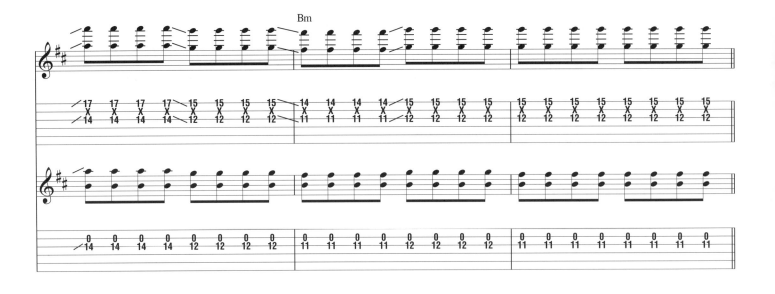

**Verse**

Gtr. 2 tacet

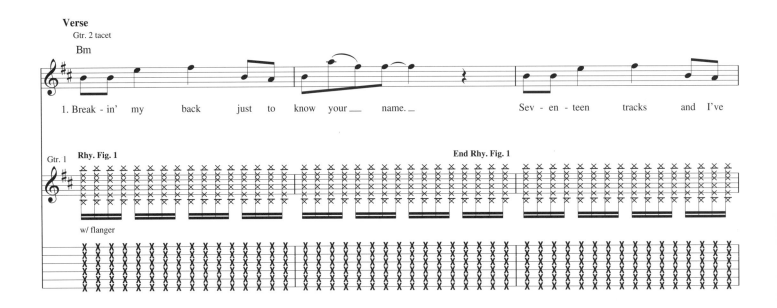

1. Break - in' my back just to know your ___ name. ___ Sev - en - teen tracks and I've

Gtr. 1 **Rhy. Fig. 1**

**End Rhy. Fig. 1**

w/ flanger

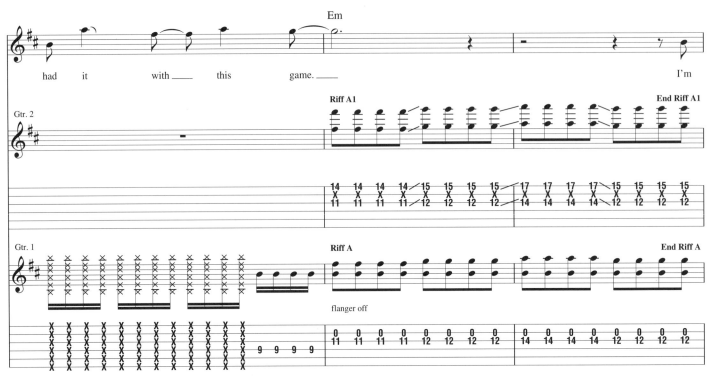

had it with ___ this game. ___ I'm

Gtr. 2 **Riff A1** **End Riff A1**

Gtr. 1 **Riff A** **End Riff A**

flanger off

Gtr. 1: w/ Rhy. Fig. 1 (3 times)
Gtr. 2 tacet

break-in' my back just to know your ___ name, ___ but heav-en ain't close ___ in a place like ___ this. ___

Gtrs. 1 & 2: w/ Riffs A & A1

An - y-thing goes, but don't ___ blink, ___ you ___ might miss. _____ 'Cause

Gtr. 1: w/ Rhy. Fig. 1 (2 times)

heav-en ain't close ___ in a place like ___ this. I said, uh, heav-en ain't close ___ in a place like ___ this. ___

**Pre-Chorus**

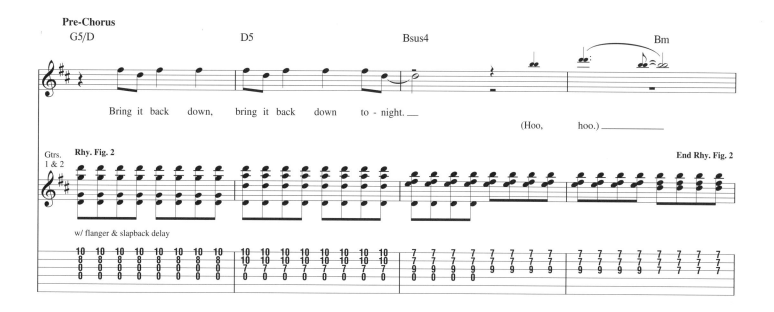

Bring it back down, bring it back down to - night. ___

(Hoo, hoo.) _____

Gtrs. 1 & 2 — Rhy. Fig. 2 — End Rhy. Fig. 2

w/ flanger & slapback delay

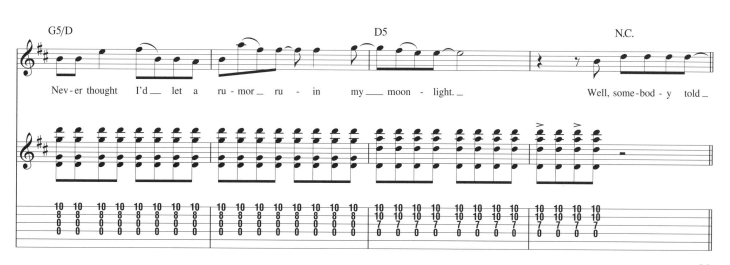

Nev - er thought I'd ___ let a ru - mor ru - in my ___ moon - light. ___ Well, some-bod - y told ___

**Chorus**

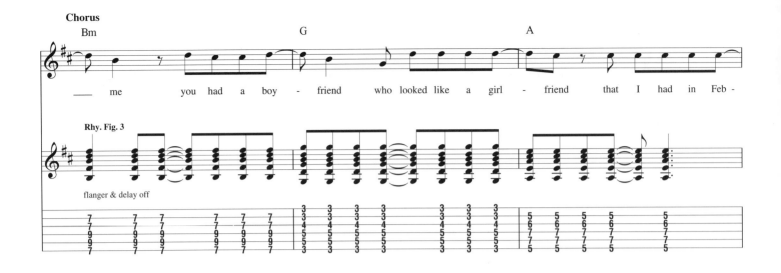

me you had a boy - friend who looked like a girl - friend that I had in Feb -

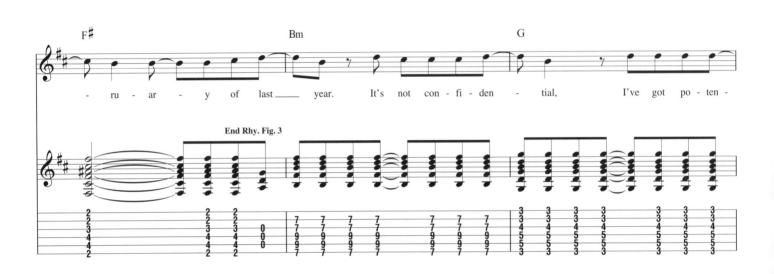

- ru - ar - y of last \_\_\_ year. It's not con - fi - den - tial, I've got po - ten -

**Verse**

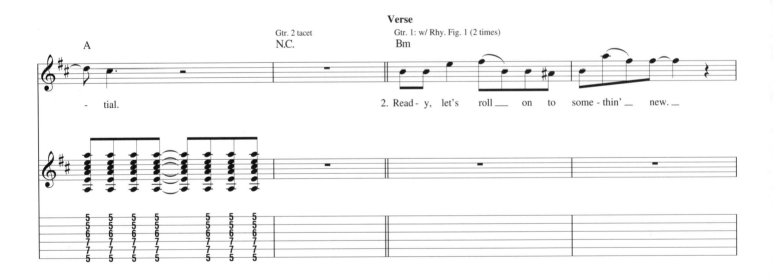

- tial. 2. Read - y, let's roll \_\_\_ on to some - thin' \_\_\_ new. \_\_\_

Tak - in' its toll \_\_\_ and I'm leav - in' \_\_\_ with - out you. \_\_\_ 'Cause

Gtr. 1: w/ Rhy. Fig. 1 (2 times)

heav-en ain't close _ in a place like _ this. I said, uh, heav-en ain't close _ in a place like this. _

**Pre-Chorus**

Gtrs. 1 & 2: w/ Rhy. Fig. 2

Bring it back down, bring it back down to-night. _____

(Hoo, hoo.) _____

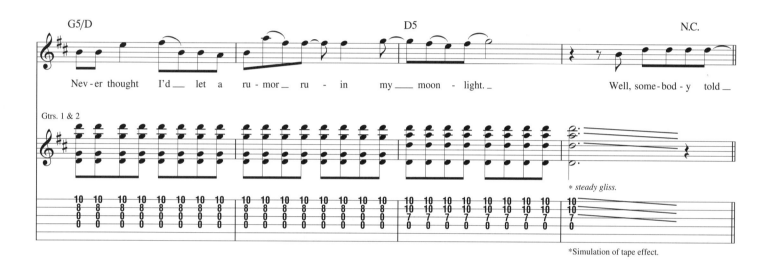

Nev-er thought I'd _ let a ru-mor ru-in my _ moon-light. _ Well, some-bod-y told _

Gtrs. 1 & 2

*steady gliss.

*Simulation of tape effect.

**Chorus**

Gtrs. 1 & 2: w/ Rhy. Fig. 3 (1 1/2 times)

_ me you had a boy-friend who looked like a girl-friend that I had in Feb-ru-ar-y of last _

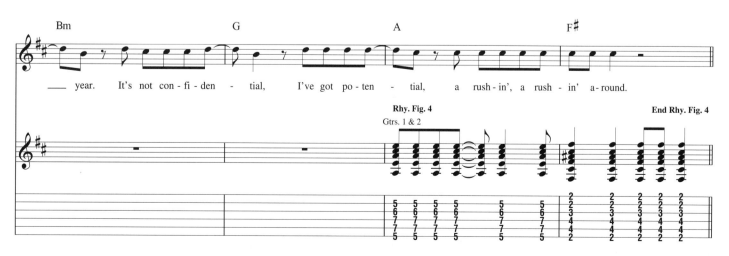

_ year. It's not con-fi-den - tial, I've got po-ten-tial, a rush-in', a rush-in' a-round.

Rhy. Fig. 4          End Rhy. Fig. 4

Gtrs. 1 & 2

25

**Chorus**

me you had a boy - friend who looked like a girl - friend that I had in Feb -

- ru - ar - y of last ___ year. It's not con - fi - den - tial, I've got po - ten -

1. - tial, a rush - in', a rush - in' a - round. Now some - bod - y told ___

2. - tial, a rush - in', a rush -

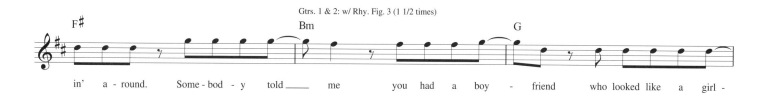

in' a - round. Some - bod - y told ___ me you had a boy - friend who looked like a girl -

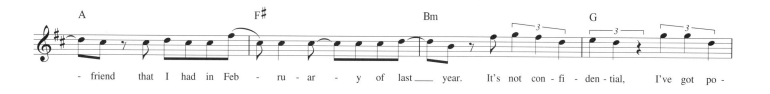

- friend that I had in Feb - ru - ar - y of last ___ year. It's not con - fi - den - tial, I've got po -

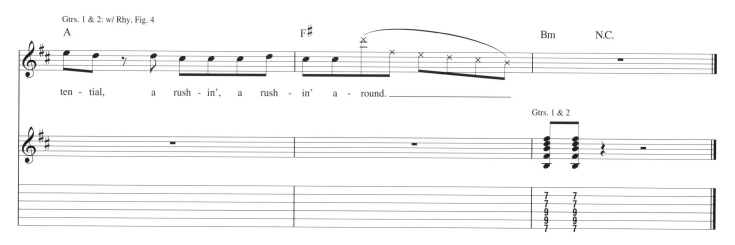

ten - tial, a rush - in', a rush - in' a - round. ___

# All These Things That I've Done

**Words and Music by Brandon Flowers, Dave Keuning, Mark Stoermer and Ronnie Vannucci**

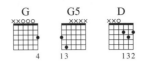

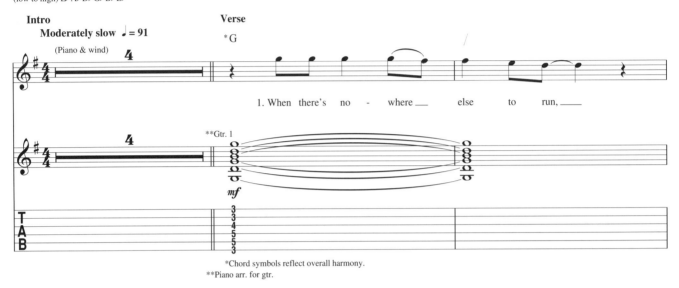

*Chord symbols reflect overall harmony.
**Piano arr. for gtr.

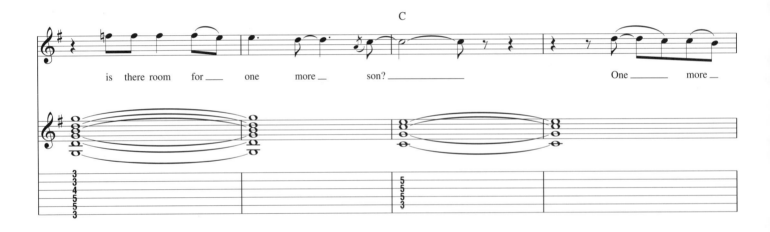

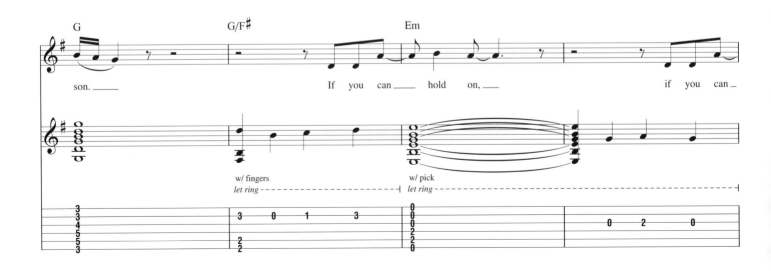

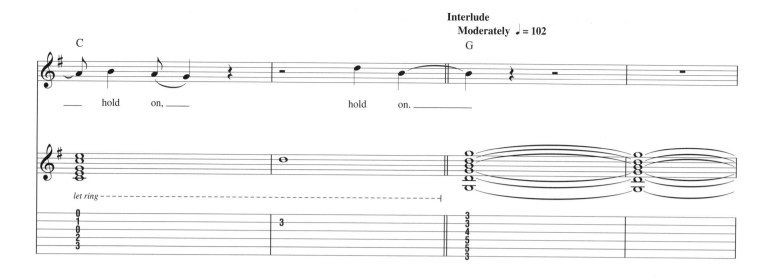

hold on, ___ hold on. ___

let ring - - - - - - - - - - - - - - - - - - - - - - - - - - - - - - - - -

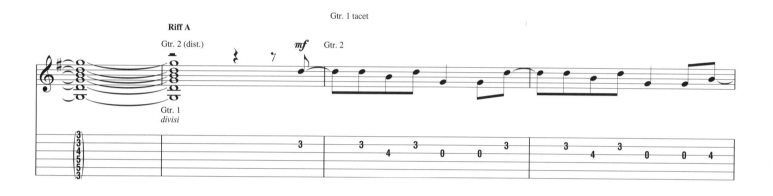

Gtr. 1 tacet

Riff A

Gtr. 2 (dist.)

*mf*  Gtr. 2

Gtr. 1
*divisi*

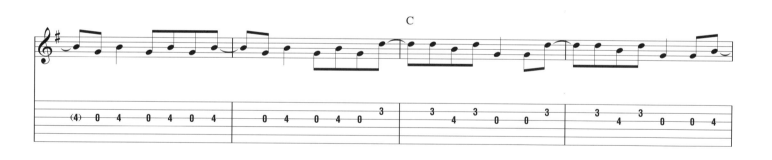

Verse

2. I wan-na stand up. ___ I wan-na let go. ___

End Riff A

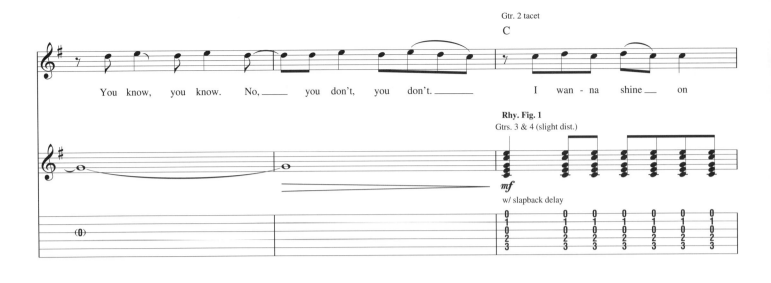

You know, you know. No, __ you don't, you don't. __ I wan-na shine __ on

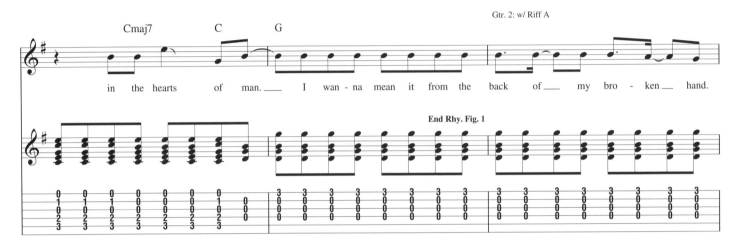

in the hearts of man. __ I wan-na mean it from the back of __ my bro-ken __ hand.

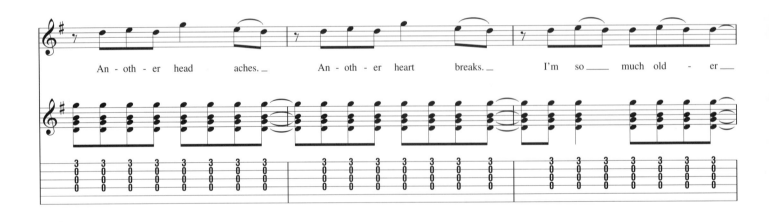

An-oth-er head aches. __ An-oth-er heart breaks. __ I'm so __ much old-er __

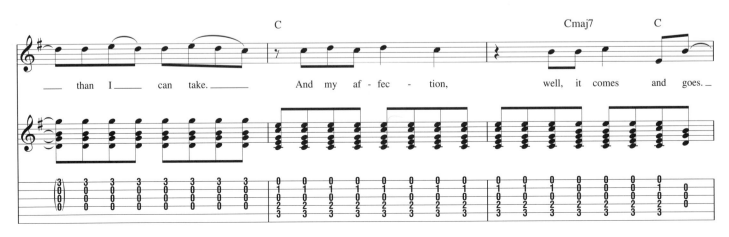

__ than I __ can take. __ And my af-fec-tion, well, it comes and goes. __

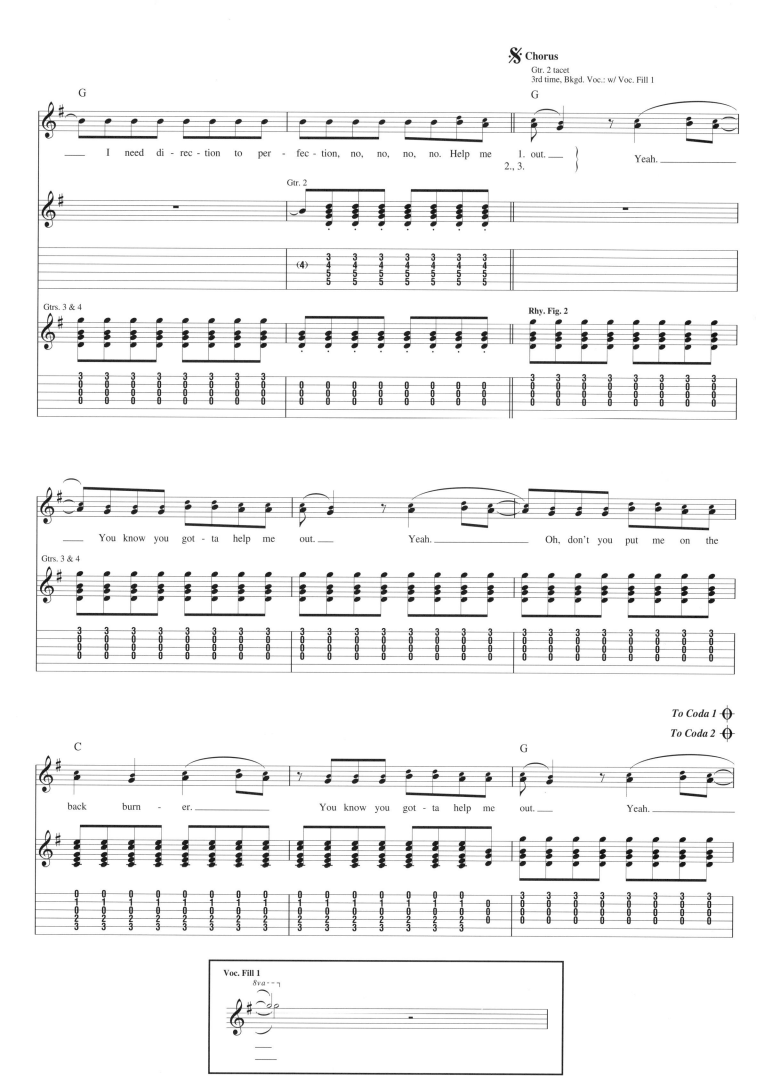

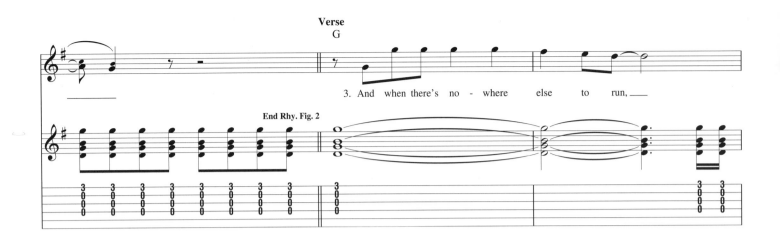

**Verse**

3. And when there's no - where else to run,

Gtr. 2: w/ Riff A (1st 3 meas.)

Gtrs. 3 & 4: w/ Rhy. Fig. 1

is there room for one more ____ son? These chang - es ain't

Cmaj7    C    G

*D.S. al Coda 1*

Gtrs. 3 & 4

chang - ing me. ____ The cold - heart - ed boy I used to be. ____

Gtr. 2

**⊕ Coda 1**

Em

____ You're gon - na bring your - self down.  Yeah. ____  You're gon - na bring your - self

Rhy. Fig. 3

32

Gtr. 3: w/ Rhy. Fig. 2 (1st 4 meas.)

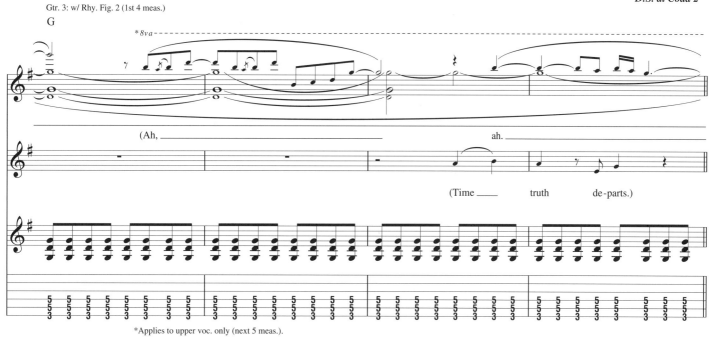

(Ah, _____ ah. _____)

(Time ____ truth de-parts.)

*Applies to upper voc. only (next 5 meas.).

⊕ Coda 2

Gtrs. 3 & 4: w/ Rhy. Fig. 2

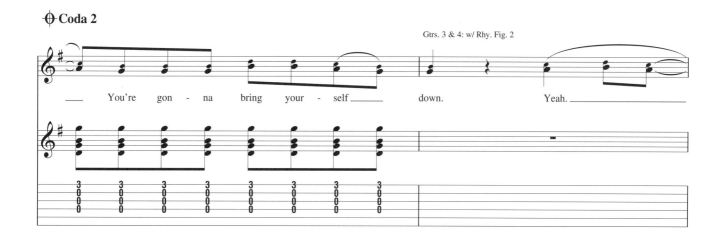

____ You're gon - na bring your - self ____ down. Yeah. _____

____ You're gon - na bring your - self ____ down. Yeah. _____ Oh, don't you put me on the

back burn - er. _____ You're gon - na bring your - self ____ down. Yeah. _____

Gtrs. 3 & 4: w/ Rhy. Fig. 3 (1st 2 meas.)

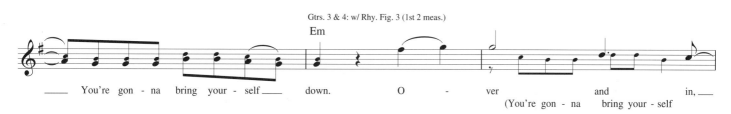

____ You're gon - na bring your - self ____ down. O - ver and in, ____
(You're gon - na bring your - self

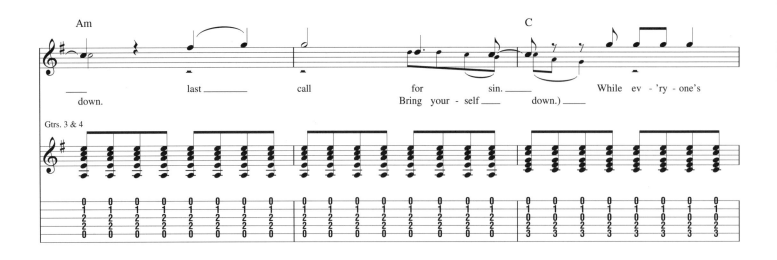

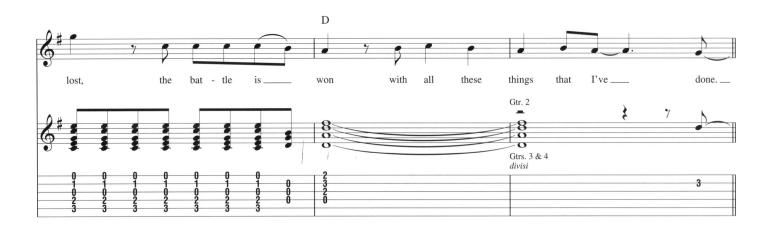

**Outro**

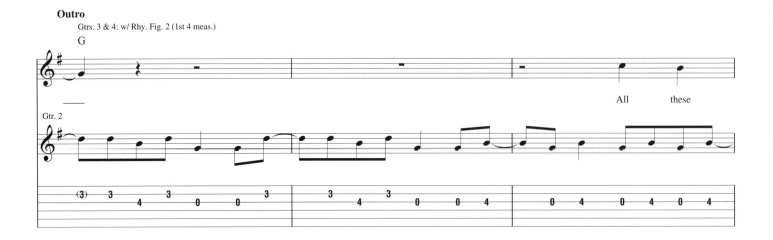

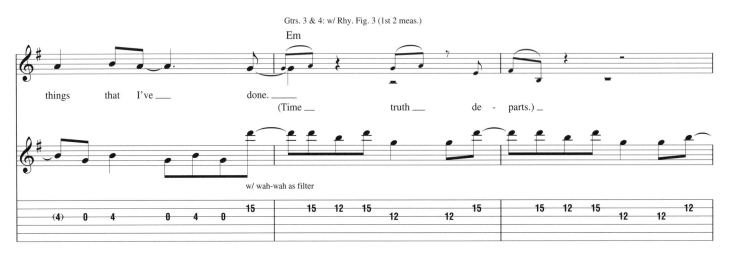

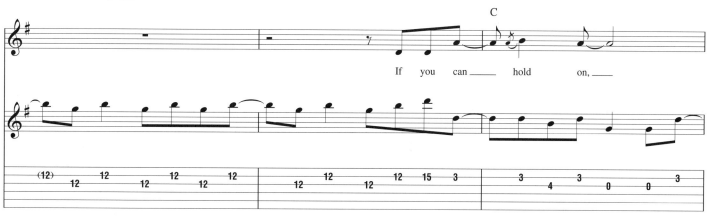

If you can ___ hold on, ___

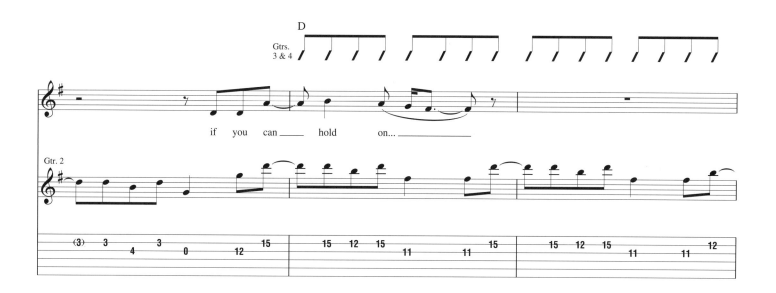

if you can ___ hold on... ___

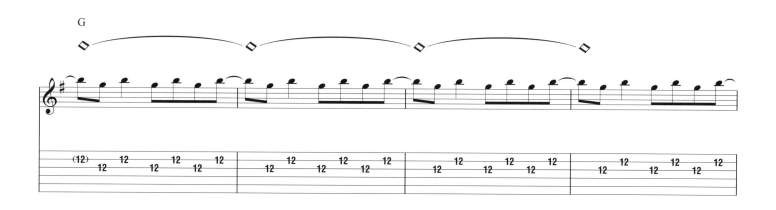

Gtrs. 3 & 4 tacet

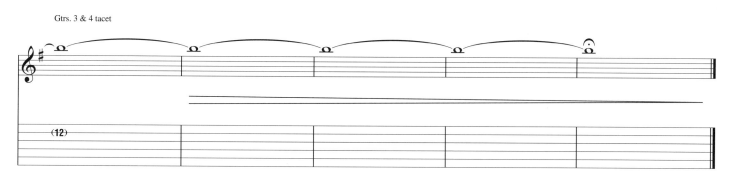

# Andy, You're a Star

**Words and Music by Brandon Flowers, Dave Keuning, Mark Stoermer and Ronnie Vannucci**

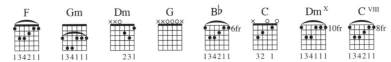

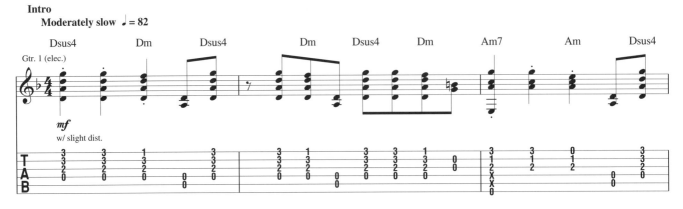

Tune down 1/2 step:
(low to high) Eb-Ab-Db-Gb-Bb-Eb

**Intro**
**Moderately slow** ♩ = 82

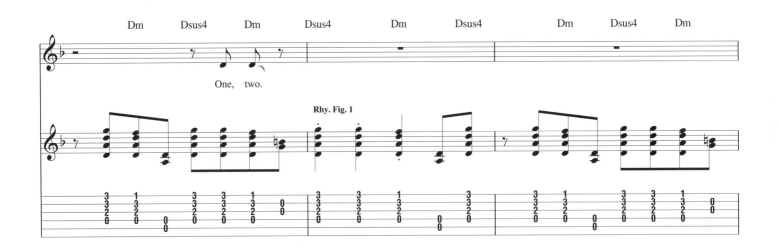

One, two.

Rhy. Fig. 1

**Verse**

Gtr. 1: w/ Rhy. Fig. 1 (2 times)

1. On the field, I re-mem-ber you were
num-ber on the lock-er and I'll

End Rhy. Fig. 1

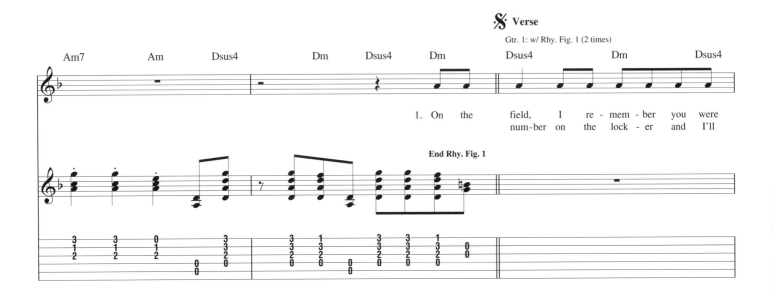

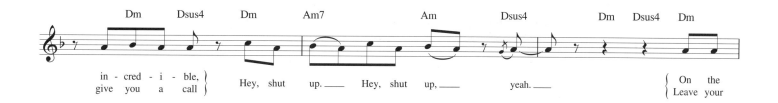

in - cred - i - ble,
give you a call

Hey, shut up. Hey, shut up, yeah. On the
Leave your

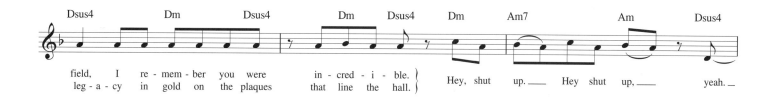

field, I re - mem - ber you were in - cred - i - ble.
leg - a - cy in gold on the plaques that line the hall.

Hey, shut up. Hey shut up, yeah.

**Pre-Chorus**

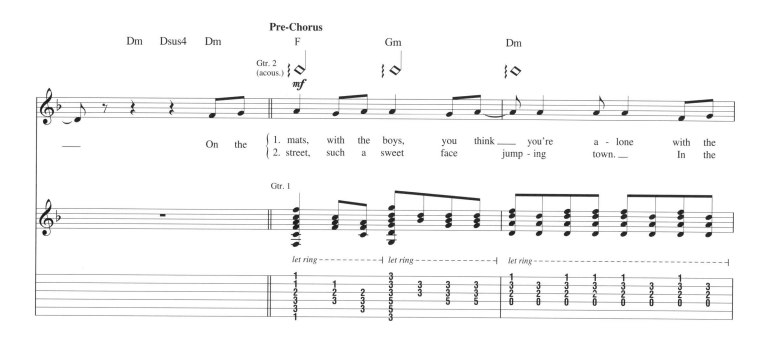

On the
1. mats, with the boys, you think you're a - lone with the
2. street, such a sweet face jump - ing town. In the

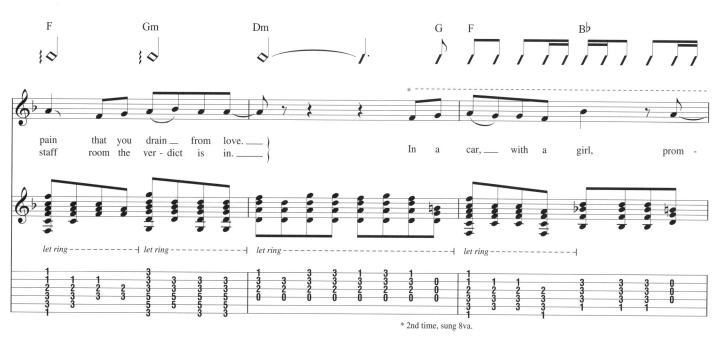

pain that you drain from love.
staff room the ver - dict is in.

In a car, with a girl, prom -

\* 2nd time, sung 8va.

39

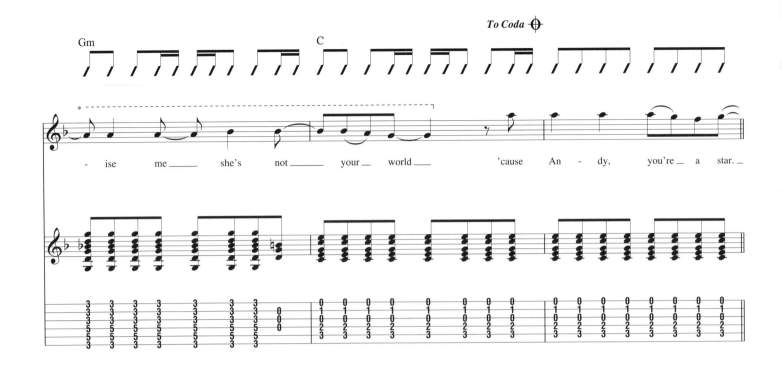

-ise me ____ she's ___ not ____ your ___ world ____ 'cause An - dy, you're ___ a star. __

**Interlude**

*D.S. al Coda*

Gtr. 1: w/ Rhy. Fig. 1
Gtr. 2 tacet

Get down, uh.

2. Leave your

⊕ **Coda**

**Chorus**
F
**Rhy. Fig. 2**

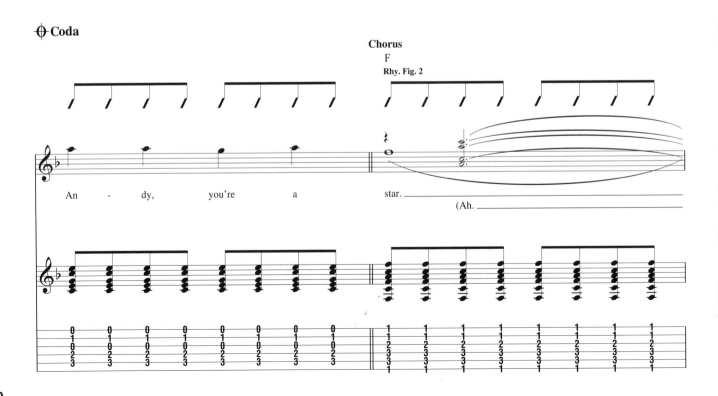

An - dy, you're a star. ____
(Ah.

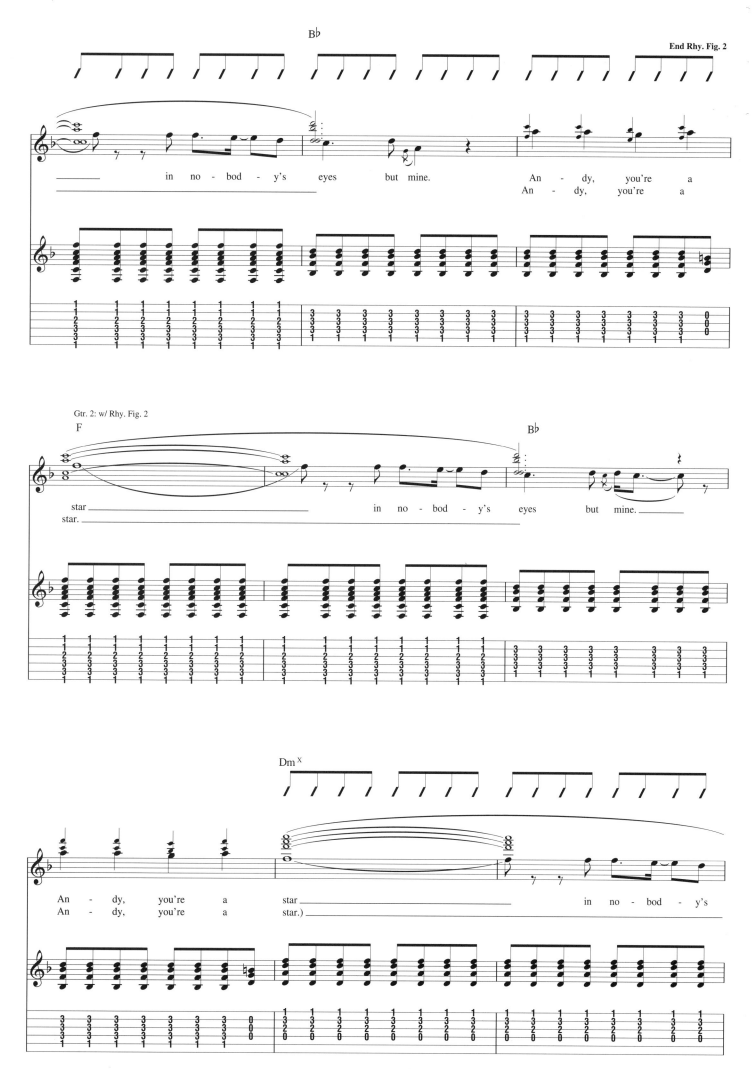

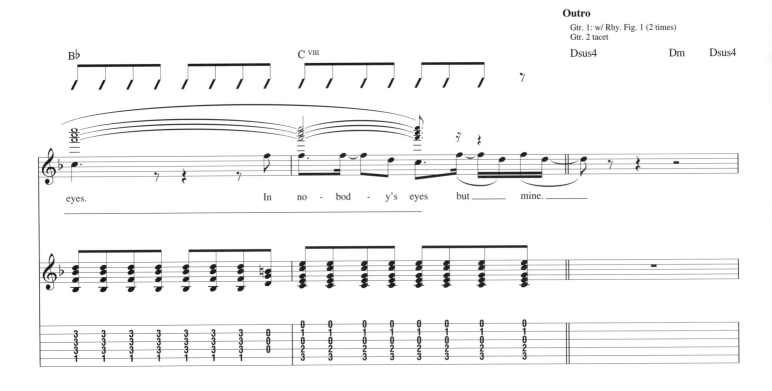

eyes.  In no - bod - y's eyes but \_\_\_\_ mine. \_\_\_\_

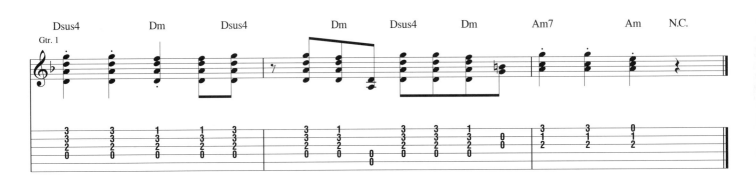

# On Top

**Words and Music by Brandon Flowers, Dave Keuning, Mark Stoermer and Ronnie Vannucci**

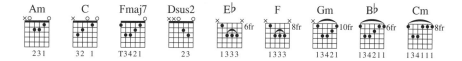

Tune down 1/2 step:
(low to high) Eb-Ab-Db-Gb-Bb-Eb

**Intro**
**Moderately** ♩ = 115

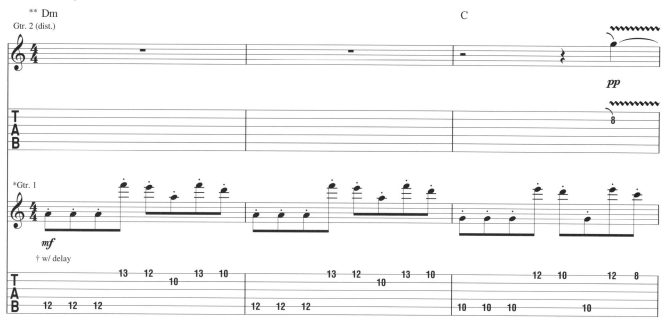

*Synth. arr. for gtr.

**Chord symbols reflect overall harmony.

† Delay set for dotted eighth-note regeneration w/ 1 repeat.

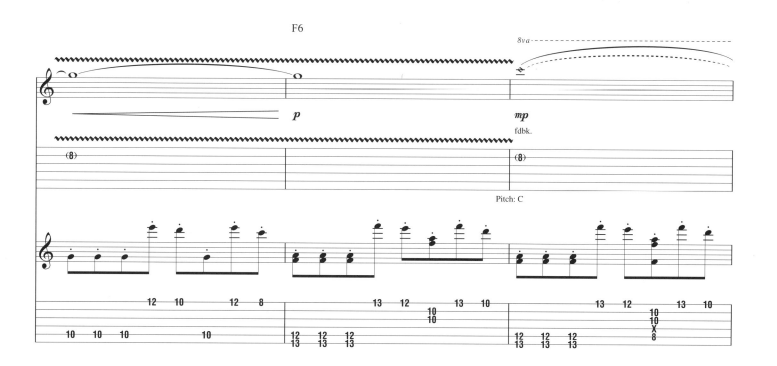

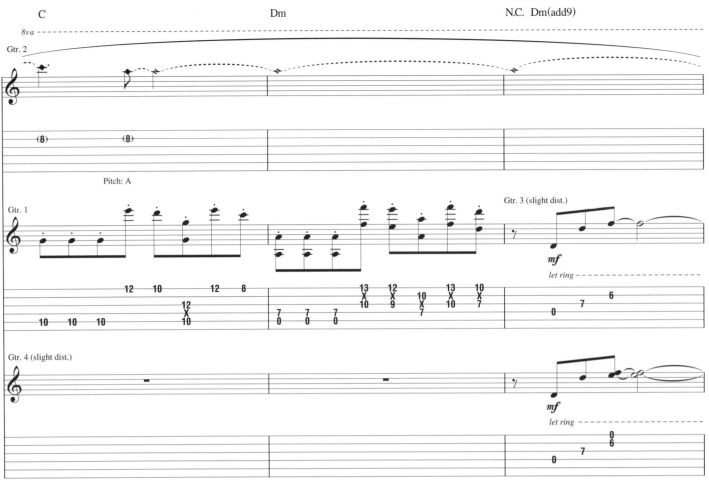

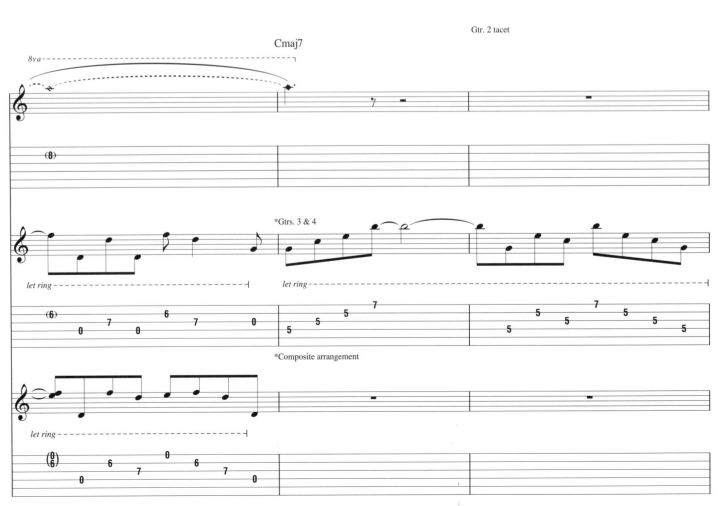

44

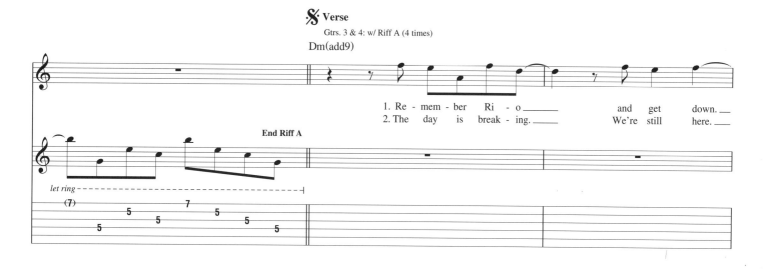

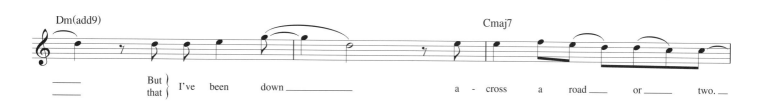

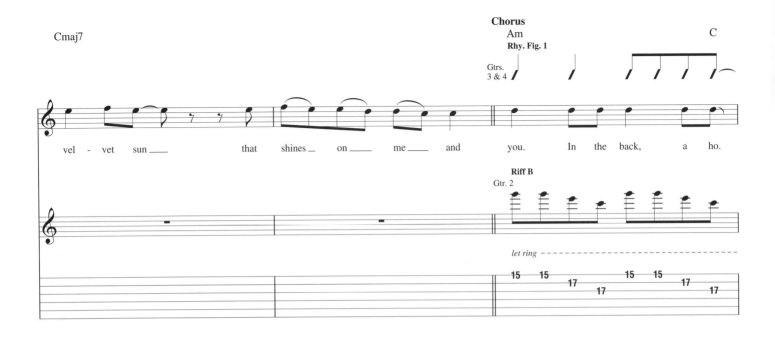

vel - vet sun ___ that shines ___ on ___ me ___ and you. In the back, a ho.

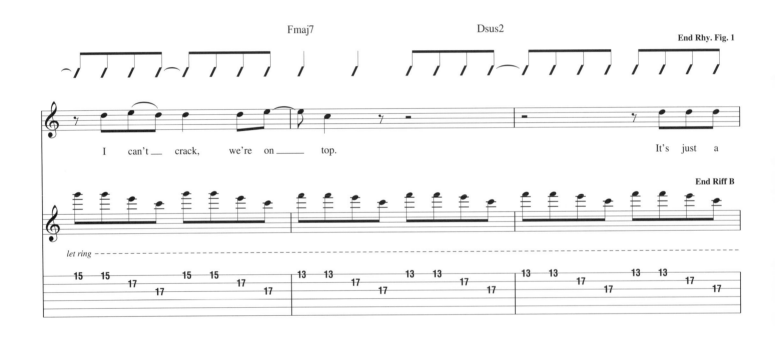

I can't ___ crack, we're on ___ top. It's just a

1st time, Gtrs. 3 & 4: w/ Rhy. Fig. 1
2nd time, Gtr. 2: w/ Riff B (2 3/4 times)
2nd time, Gtrs. 3 & 4: w/ Rhy. Fig. 1 (3 times)

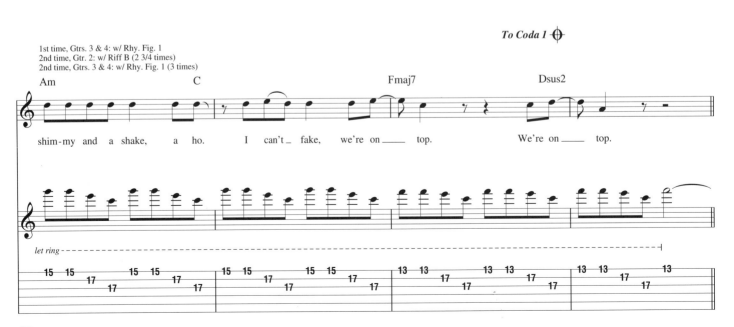

shim-my and a shake, a ho. I can't ___ fake, we're on ___ top. We're on ___ top.

**Interlude**

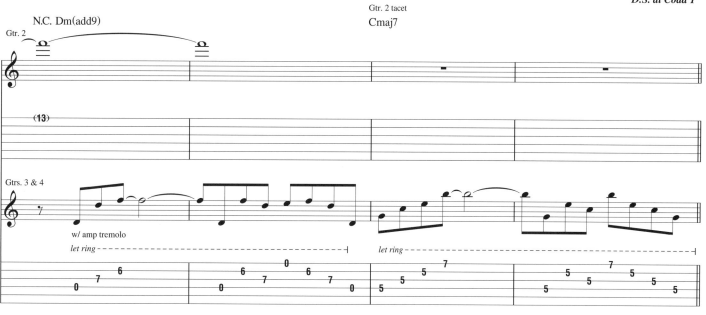

**Coda 1**

— top. We bring the bump to the grind, a ho. I don't mind, we're on —

— top. It's just a shim - my and a shake, a ho.

I can't fake, we're on — top. We're on — top.

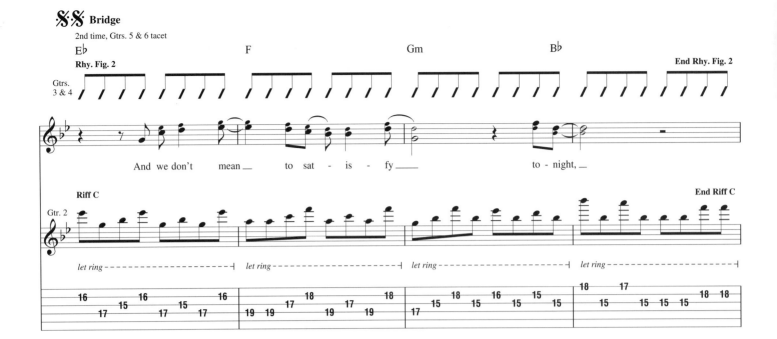

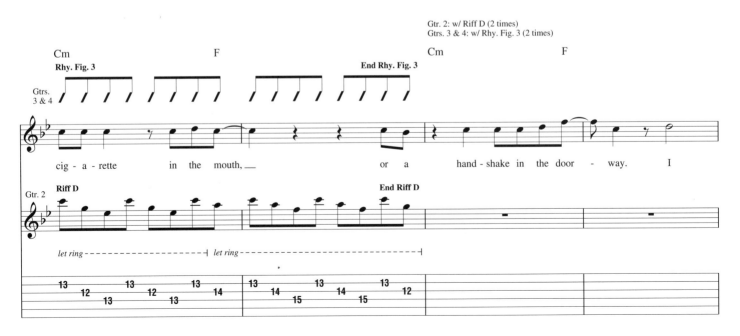

look at you ___ and smile ___ be - cause ___ I'm fine. ___

**Synth Solo**

*Gtr. 6: w/ Riff A (2 times)

Gtrs. 2, 3 & 4 tacet

Cmaj7

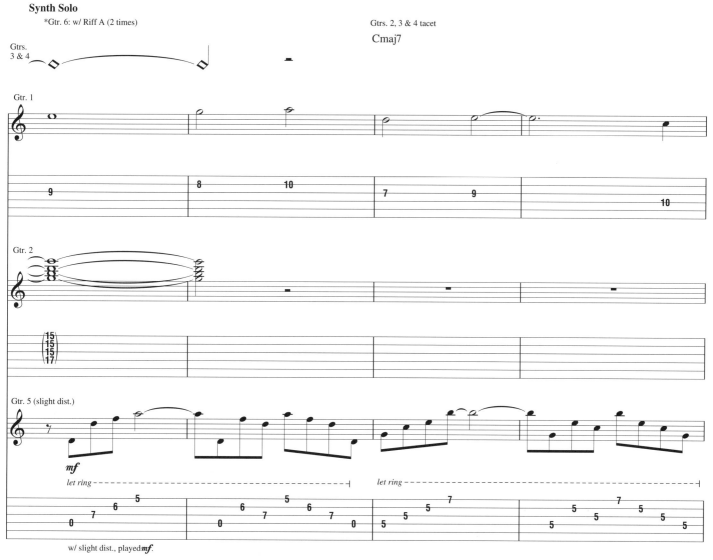

Dm(add9)                                                      Cmaj7

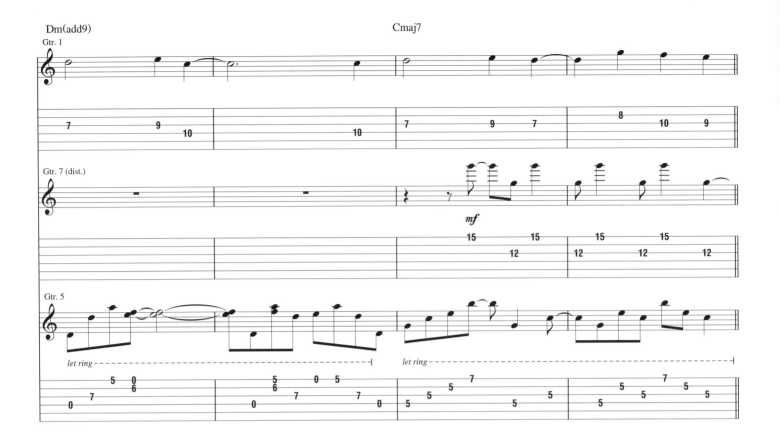

**Interlude**
Gtr. 2: w/ Riff B (1 1/2 times)
Gtrs. 3 & 4: w/ Rhy. Fig. 1 (1 1/2 times)

Am                          C                 Gtr. 7 tacet          Gtr. 1 tacet
                                                                    Fmaj7                    Dsus2

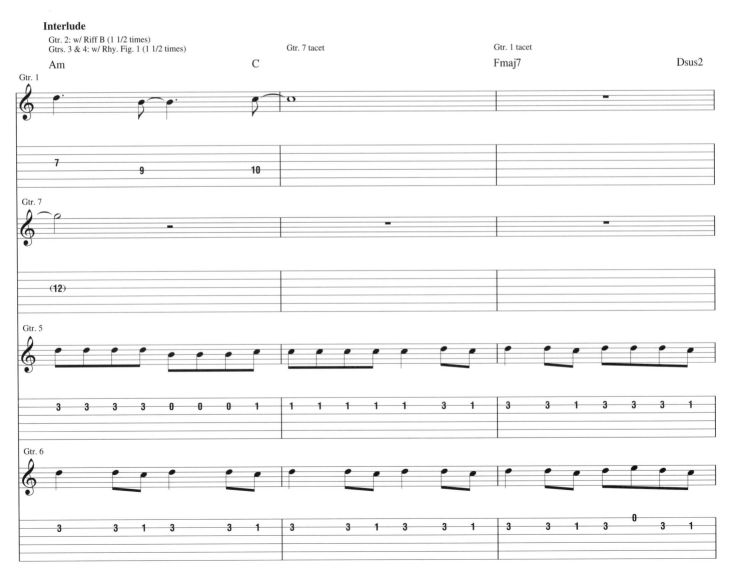

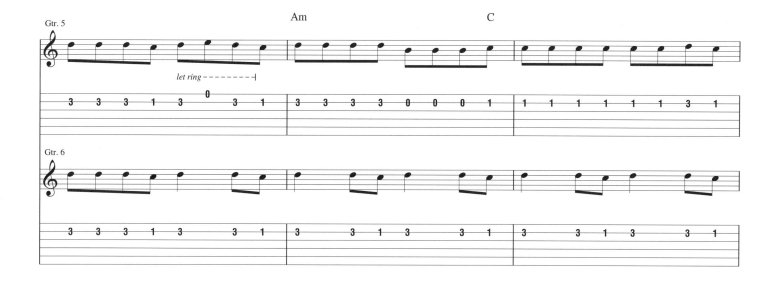

D.S.S. al Coda 2

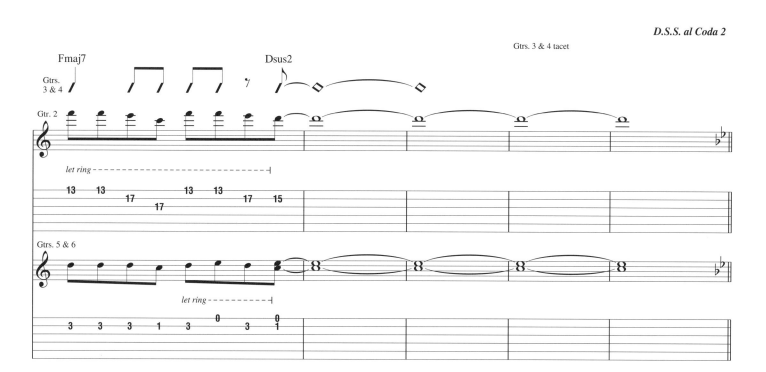

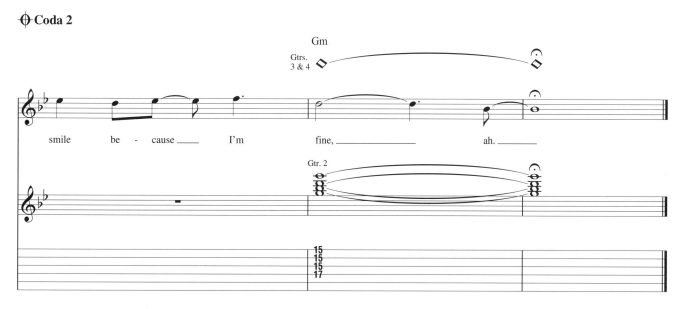

smile be - cause \_\_\_\_\_ I'm fine, _____ ah. _____

# Change Your Mind

**Words and Music by Brandon Flowers, Dave Keuning, Mark Stoermer and Ronnie Vannucci**

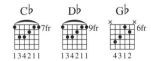

Tune down 1/2 step:
(low to high) Eb-Ab-Db-Gb-Bb-Eb

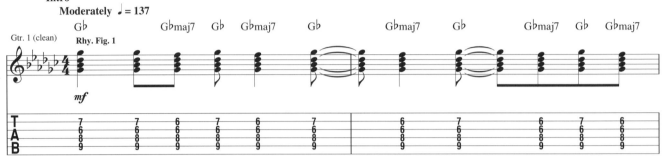

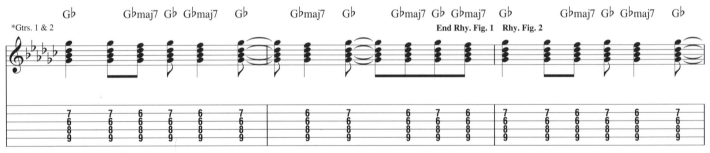

*Gtr. 2: w/ clean tone; played *mf*.

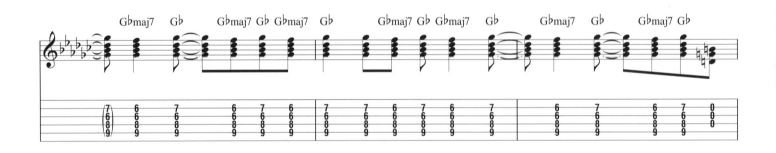

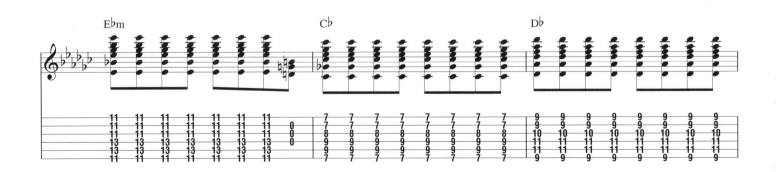

## ⊕ Coda 1

**Interlude**

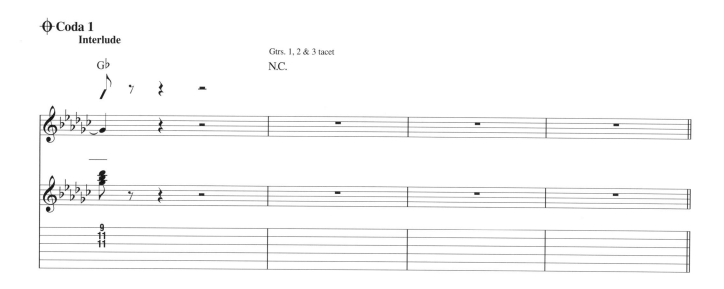

**Bridge**

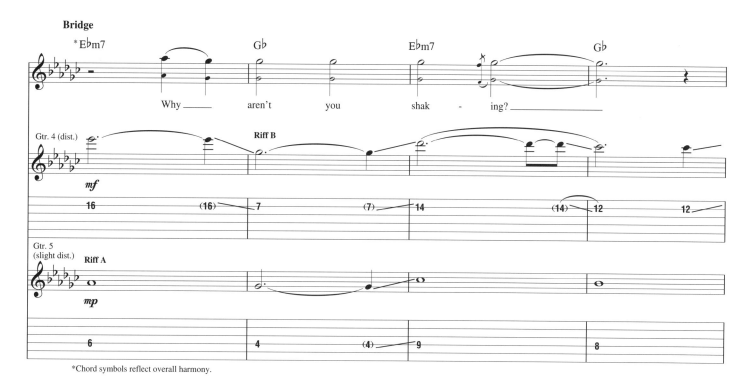

*Chord symbols reflect overall harmony.

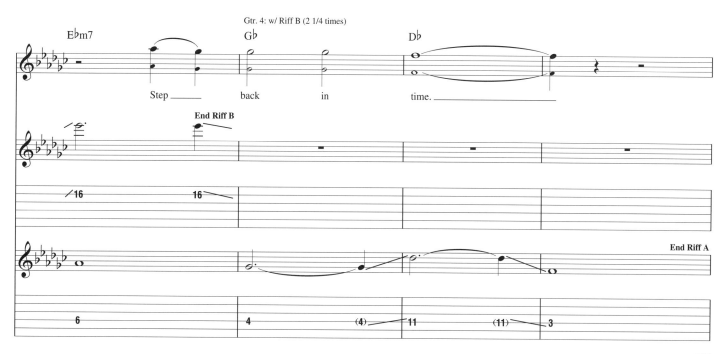

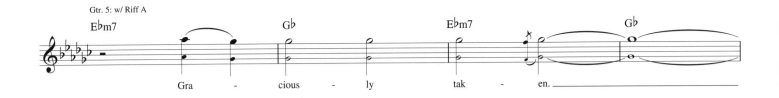

Gtr. 5: w/ Riff A

Ebm7 — Gb — Ebm7 — Gb

Gra - cious - ly tak - en. _____

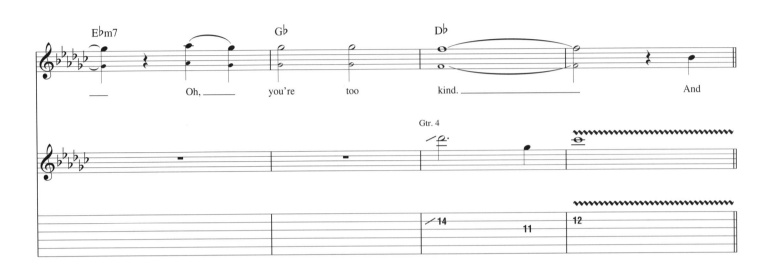

Ebm7 — Gb — Db

___ Oh, ___ you're too kind. _____ And

Gtr. 4

**Chorus**

Gtrs. 1 & 2: w/ Rhy. Fig. 3
Gtr. 3: w/ Rhy. Fig. 3A                    Gtr. 4 tacet

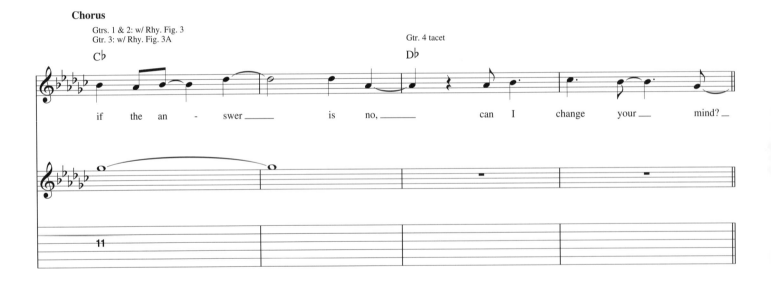

Cb — Db

if the an - swer ___ is no, ___ can I change your ___ mind? ___

**Interlude**

Gtrs. 1 & 2: w/ Rhy. Fig. 1

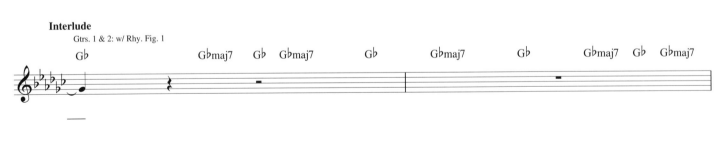

Gb   Gbmaj7  Gb  Gbmaj7    Gb    Gbmaj7    Gb    Gbmaj7  Gb  Gbmaj7

*D.S: al Coda 2*

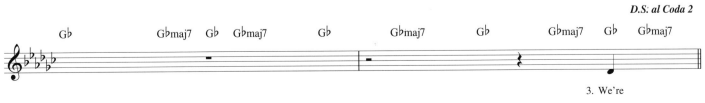

Gb   Gbmaj7  Gb  Gbmaj7    Gb    Gbmaj7    Gb    Gbmaj7  Gb  Gbmaj7

3. We're

## ⊕ Coda 2

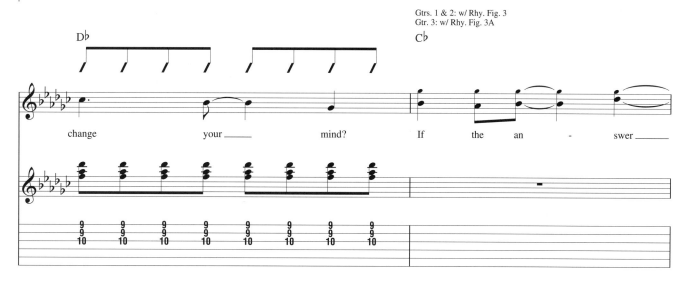

Gtrs. 1 & 2: w/ Rhy. Fig. 3
Gtr. 3: w/ Rhy. Fig. 3A

change your _____ mind? If the an - swer _____

_____ is no, _____ can I change your

## Outro

Gtrs. 1 & 2: w/ Rhy. Fig. 1

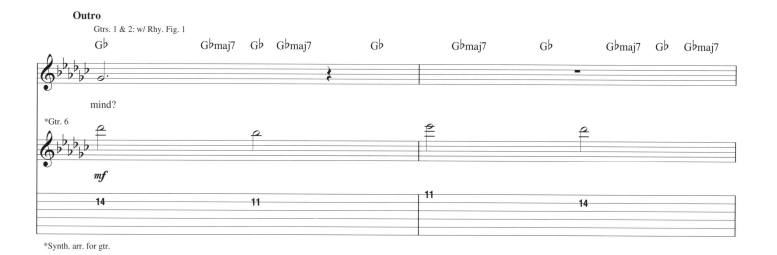

mind?

*Gtr. 6

*Synth. arr. for gtr.

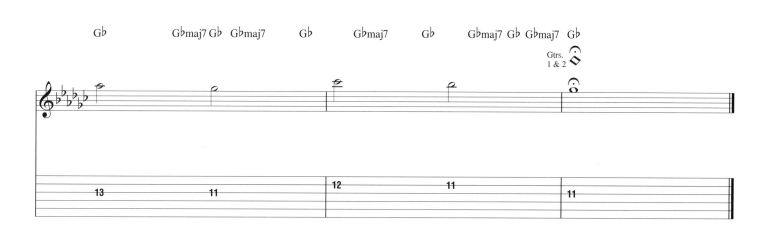

# Believe Me Natalie

**Words and Music by Brandon Flowers, Dave Keuning, Mark Stoermer and Ronnie Vannucci**

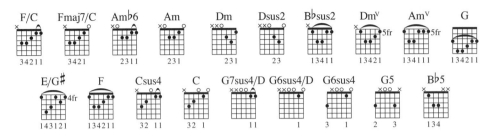

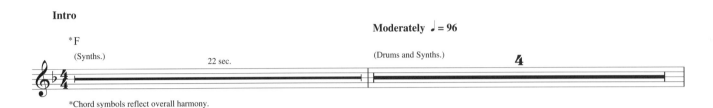

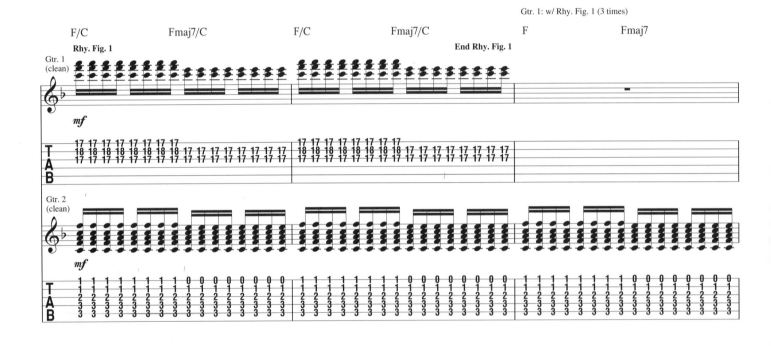

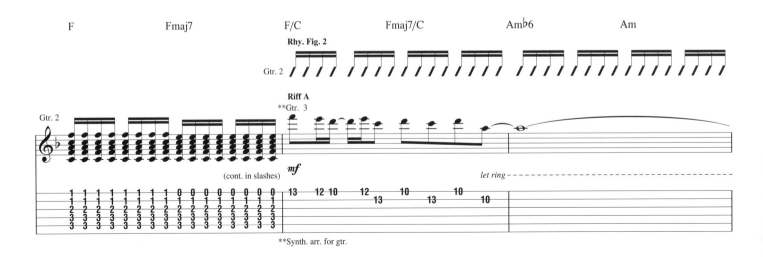

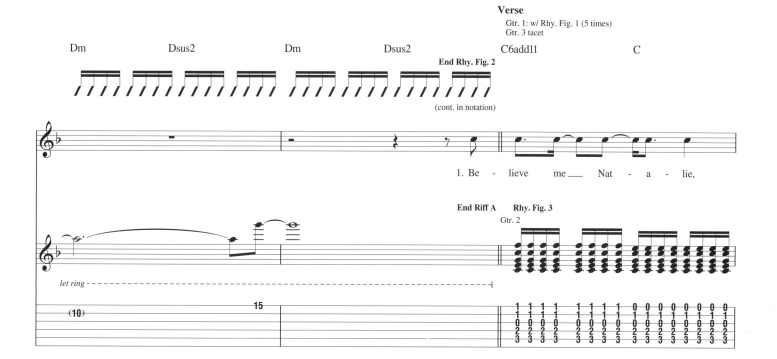

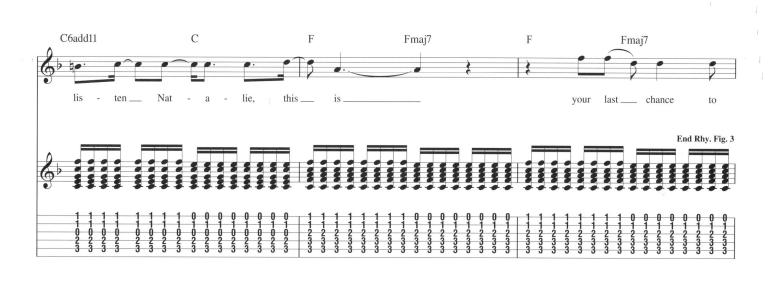

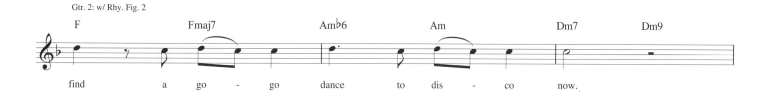

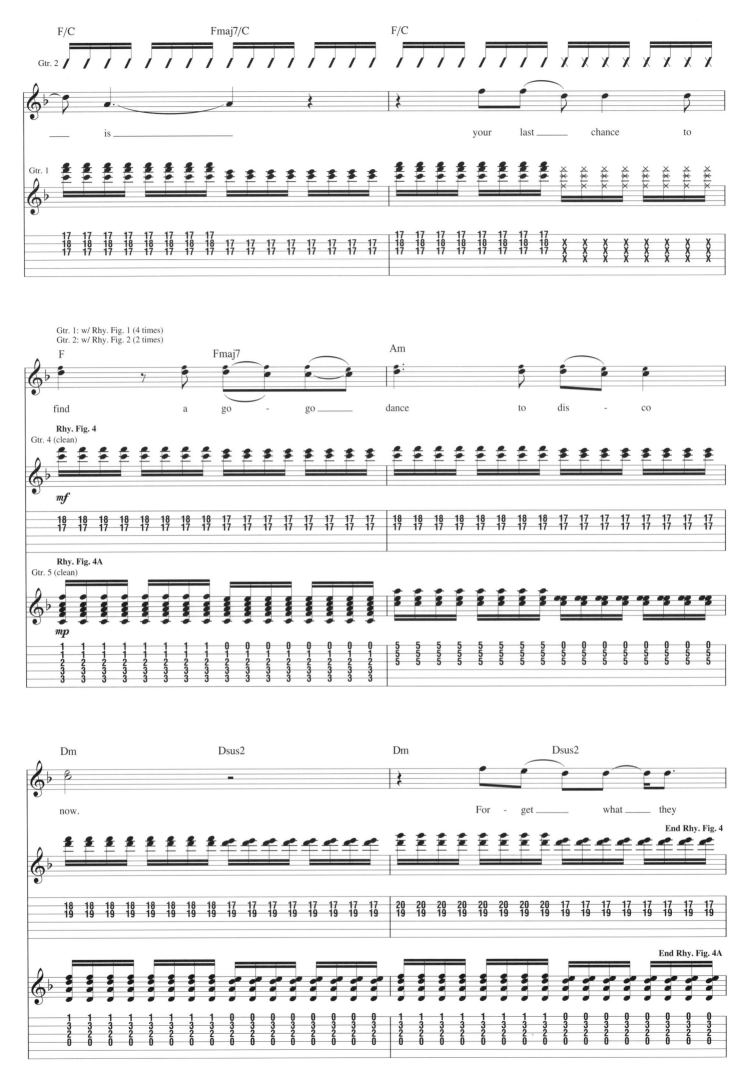

said in So- ho, leave the "Oh _____ no's" _____ out. _____

**Chorus**
**Double-time feel**

**End double-time feel**

And be- lieve _____ me, Nat - a - lie. Lis- ten _____ Nat - a - lie, this _____

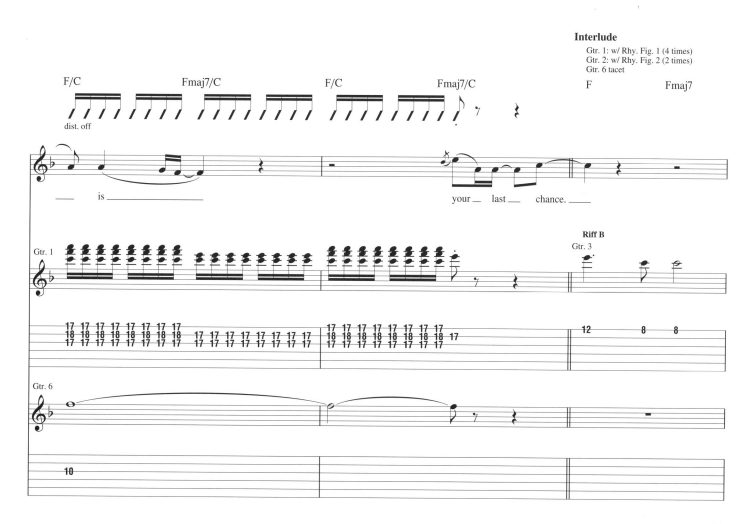

_____ is _____ is _____ your _____ last _____ chance. _____

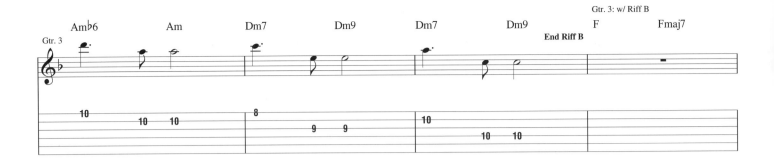

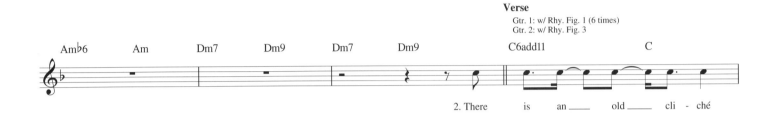

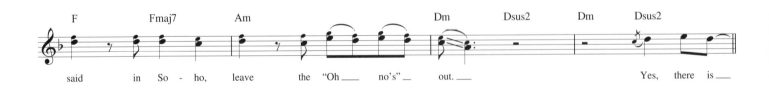

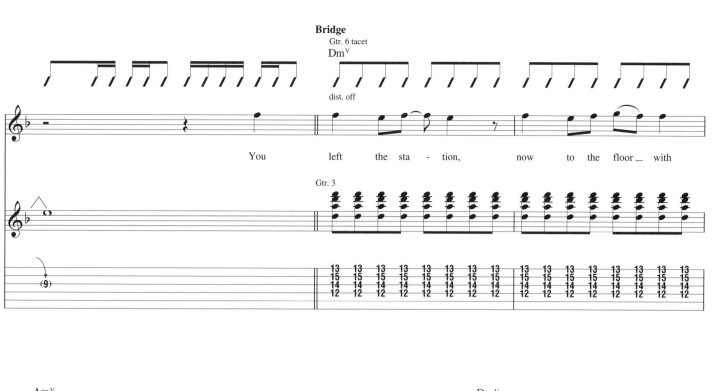

You left the sta - tion, now to the floor — with

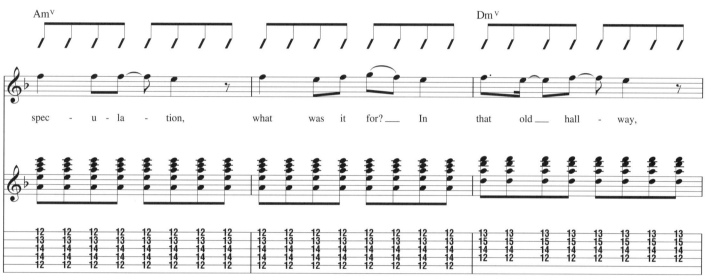

spec - u - la - tion, what was it for? — In that old — hall - way,

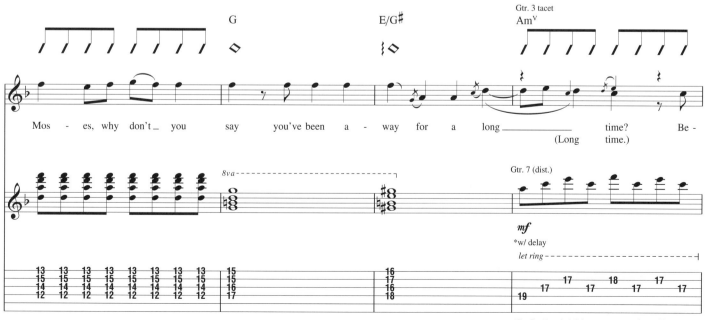

Mos - es, why don't — you say you've been a - way for a long _____ time? (Long time.) Be -

*Set for dotted eighth-note regeneration w/ 2 repeats.

lieve me ___ Nat - a - lie, this ___ is _____ your last ___ chance to

(Your last ___ chance.)
(Your last ___ chance.) ___

Gtr. 7

let ring — — — — — — — — — — — — — — — — — — — — — ┘   let ring — — — — — — — — — — — — — — — — — ┘   let ring — — — — — — — — ┘

Gtr. 1: w/ Rhy. Fig. 1 (12 times)
Gtr. 2: w/ Rhy. Fig. 2 (3 times)
Gtr. 7 tacet

F    Fmaj7    Am♭6    Am    Dm7    Dm9    Dm7    Dm9

find    a    go - go. ___      For - get ___ what ___ they

Riff D        End Riff D

*Gtr. 8

*Horns arr. for gtr.

Gtr. 3    Riff C        End Riff C

Gtr. 3: w/ Riff C (2 times)
Gtr. 8: w/ Riff D (3 times)

F    Fmaj7    Am♭6    Am    Dm7    Dm9    Dm7    Dm9

said    in    So - ho. _____        And

walk a-way _____ if my dreams for us __ can't get __ you through __ just one _

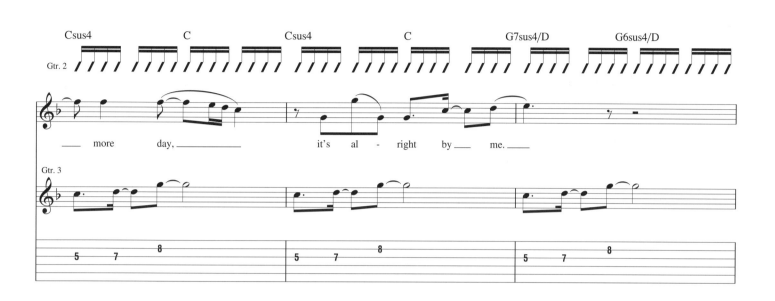

__ more day, _____ it's al-right by __ me. _____

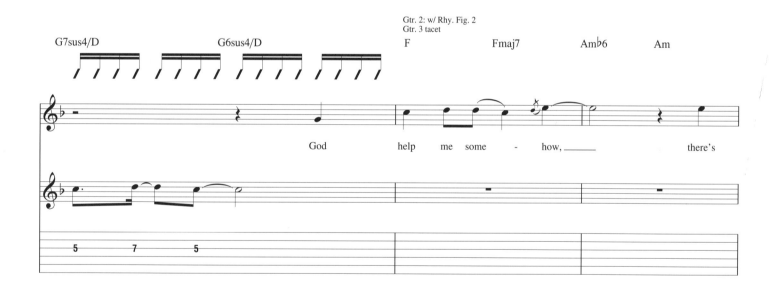

God help me some - how, _____ there's

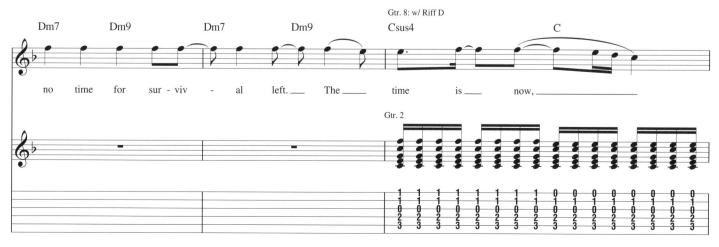

no time for sur-viv - al left. The __ time is __ now, _____

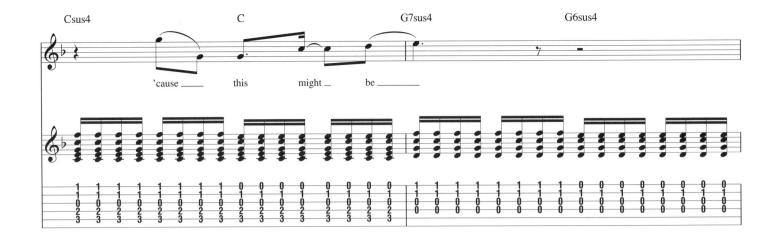

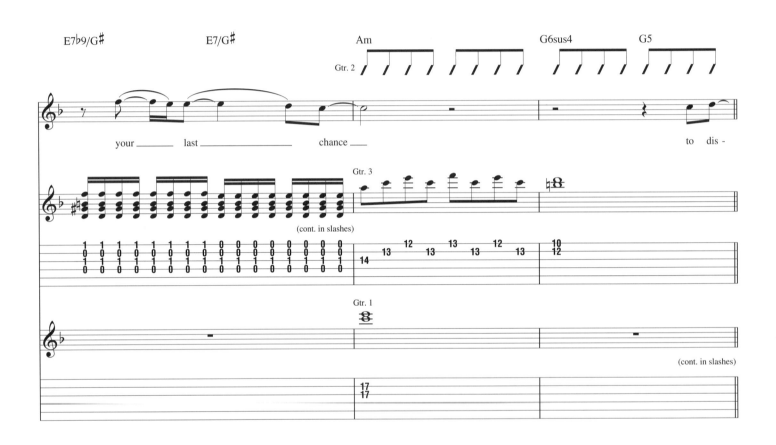

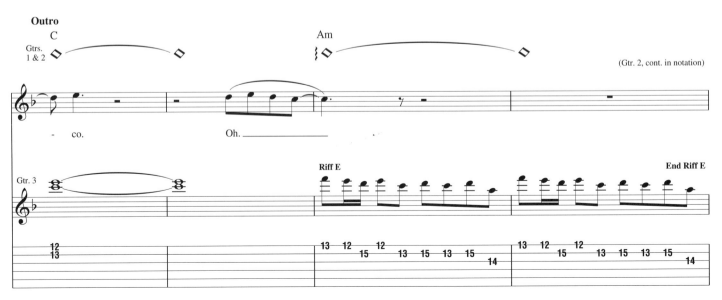

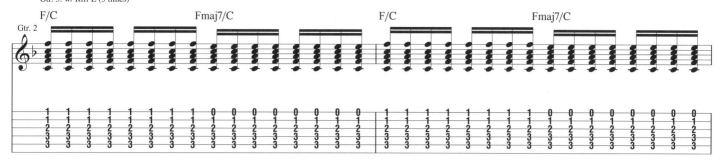

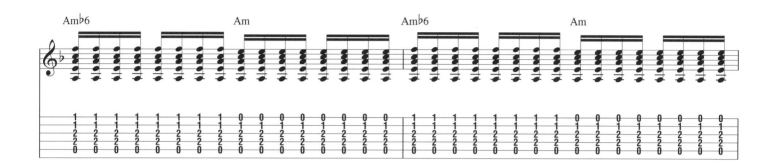

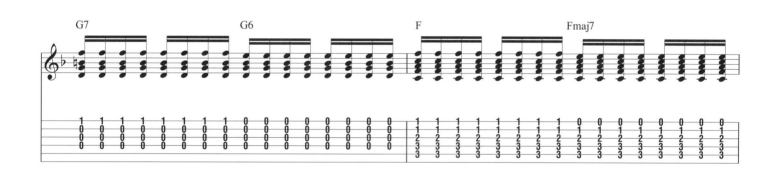

*Fade out*

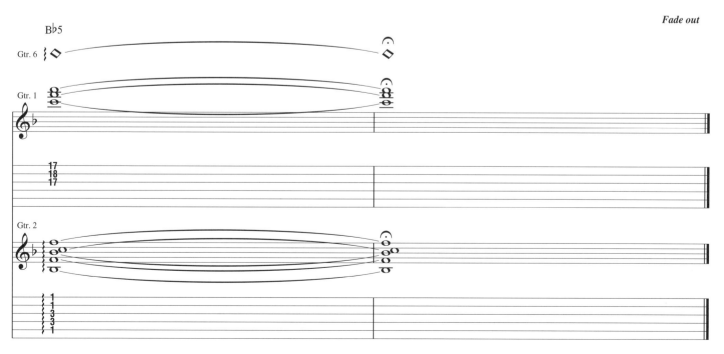

# Midnight Show

**Words and Music by Brandon Flowers, Dave Keuning, Mark Stoermer and Ronnie Vannucci**

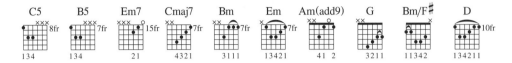

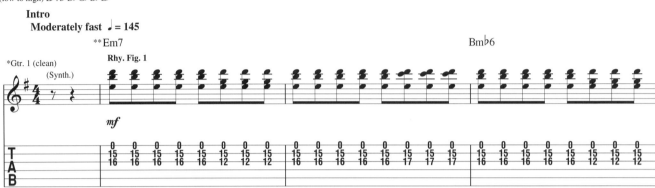

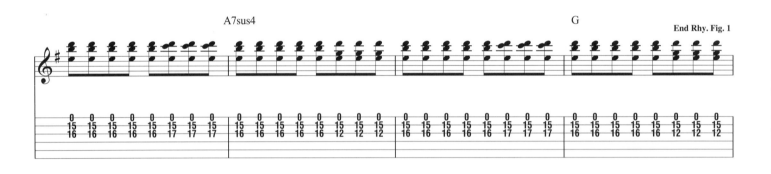

*Doubled throughout   **Chord symbols reflect overall harmony.

† Bass plays D.

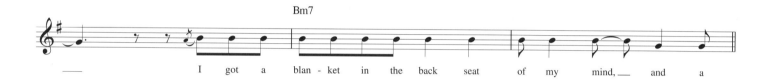

### Pre-Chorus

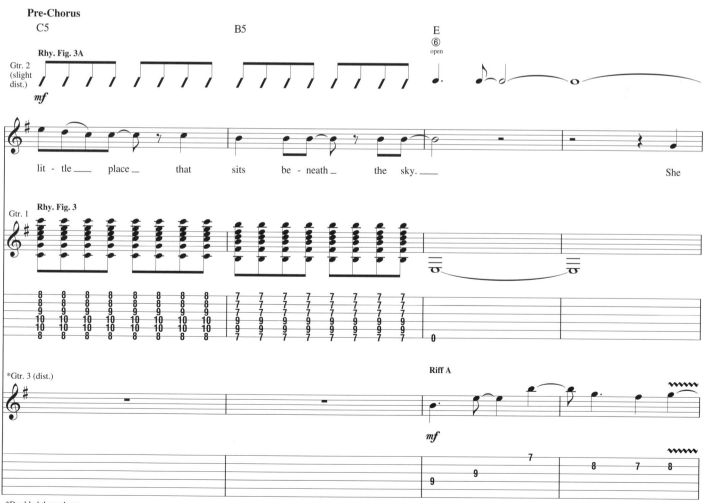

*Doubled throughout.

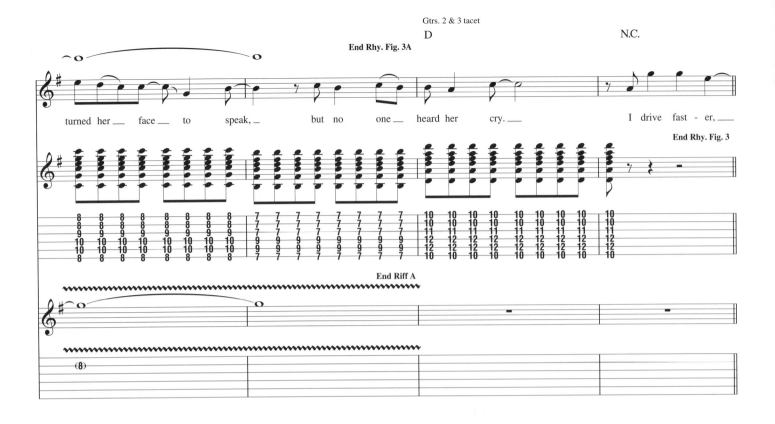

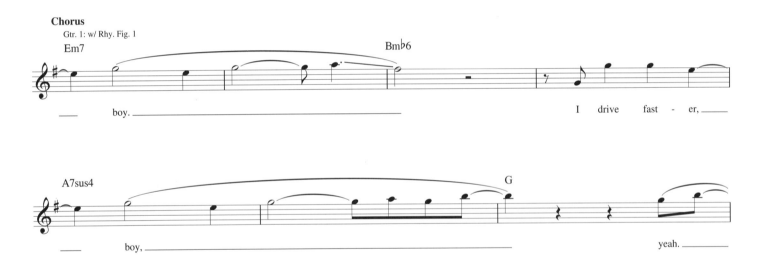

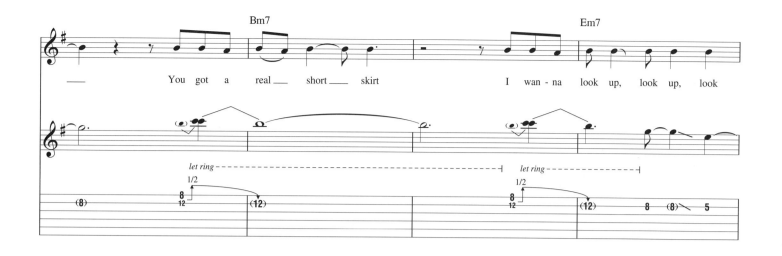

You got a real short skirt I wan-na look up, look up, look

*let ring*

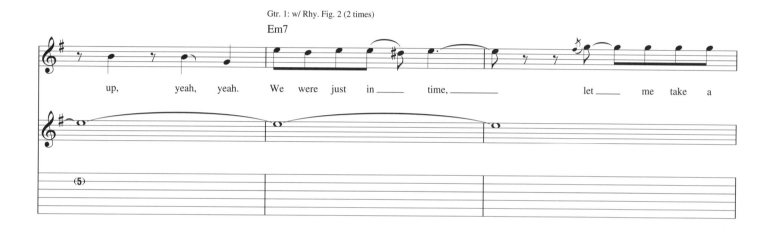

Gtr. 1: w/ Rhy. Fig. 2 (2 times)

up, yeah, yeah. We were just in time, let me take a

Gtr. 3 tacet

lit-tle more off your mind. There's some-thing in my head,

some-where in the back say-in' we were just a good thing, we were such a good thing.

**Pre-Chorus**

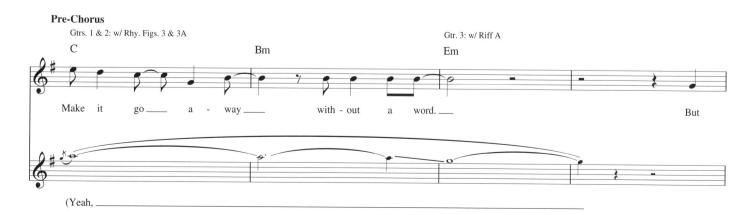

Gtrs. 1 & 2: w/ Rhy. Figs. 3 & 3A

Gtr. 3: w/ Riff A

Make it go a-way with-out a word. But

(Yeah,

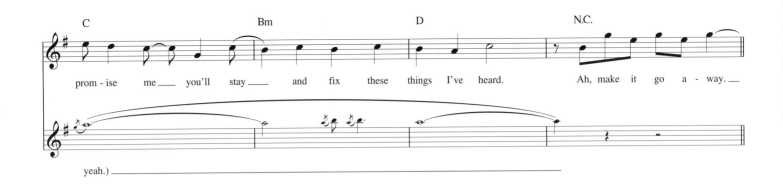

**C**          **Bm**          **D**          **N.C.**

prom - ise me \_\_\_ you'll stay \_\_\_ and fix these things I've heard.     Ah, make it go a - way. \_\_\_

yeah.) _____

**Chorus**

Gtr. 1: w/ Rhy. Fig. 1

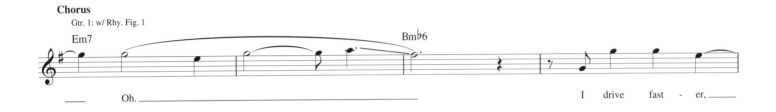

**Em7**                        **Bm♭6**

\_\_\_ Oh. _____ I drive fast - er, \_\_\_

Gtr. 1: w/ Rhy. Fill 1

**A7sus4**                   **G**          **G/D**

\_\_\_ boy, _____ yeah. \_\_\_\_\_ Oh, \_\_\_ no. \_\_\_

**Guitar Solo**

**E5**                                  **B5**

Gtr. 3

**A5**                                **G5**

**Bridge**

Oh, crash-ing time ___ can't hide a guilt - y girl. ___

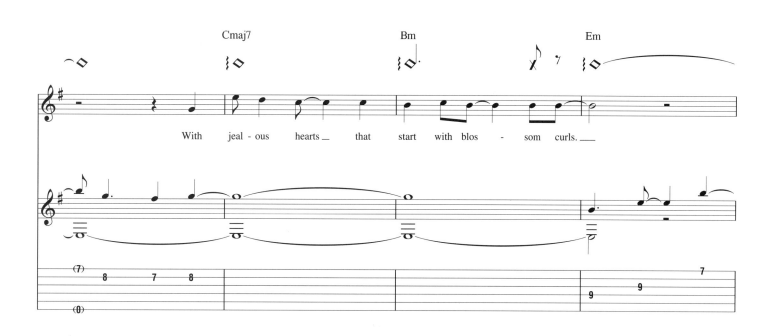

With jeal - ous hearts ___ that start with blos - som curls. ___

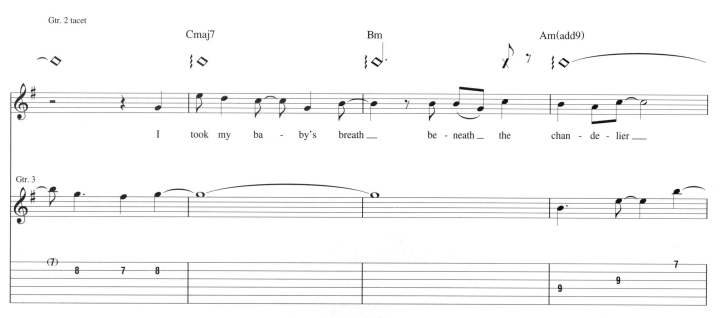

I took my ba - by's breath ___ be - neath ___ the chan - de - lier ___

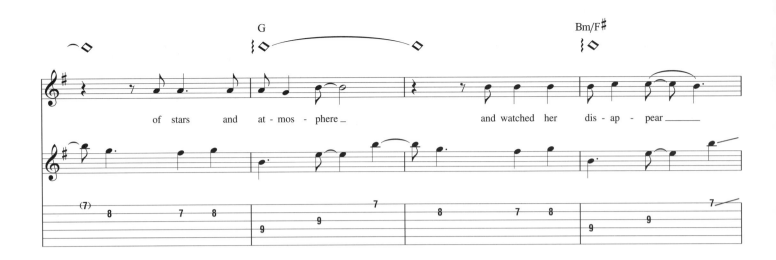

of stars and at - mos - phere _ and watched her dis - ap - pear _

**Chorus**
Gtr. 1: w/ Rhy. Fig. 1 (1st 4 meas.) (6 times)     Gtr. 3 tacet

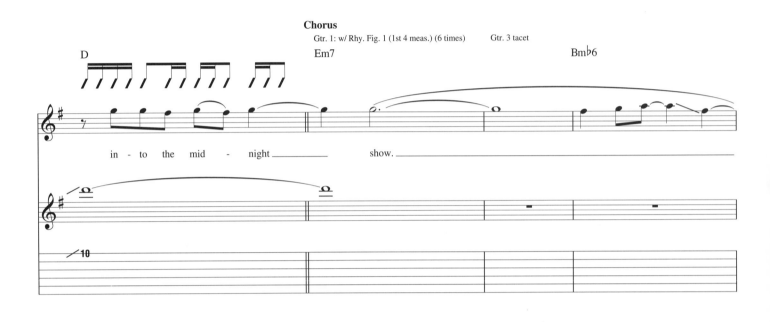

in - to the mid - night _ show. _

_ Ah fast - er, ah fast - er, ah fast - er, ah fast - er, fast - er,

ah, fast - er. Oh, no, no, _ no, _ no, no, no. No, no, _ no, _

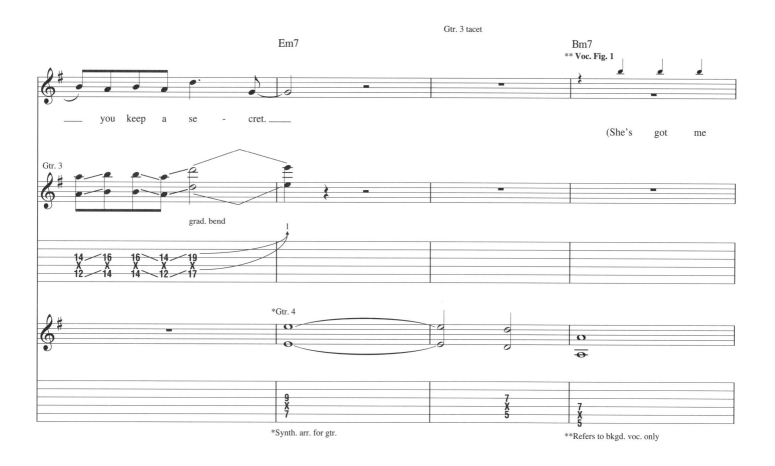

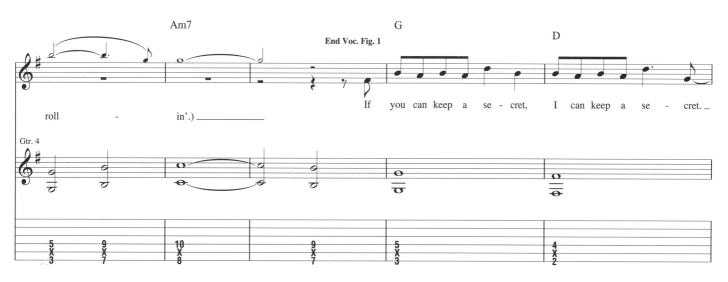

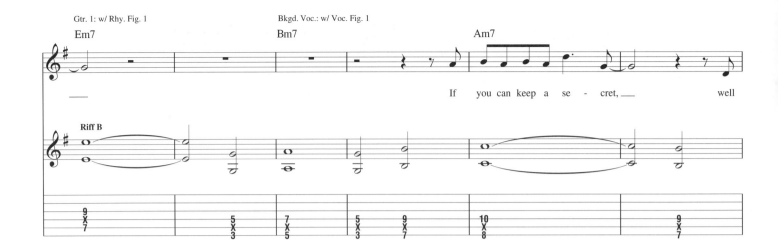

**Outro**
**Freely**

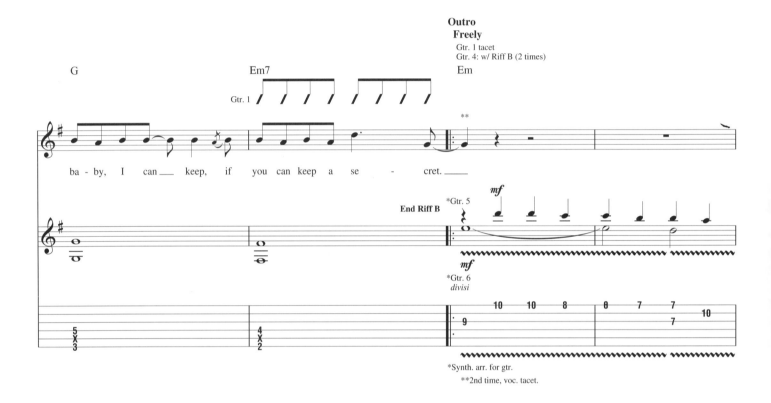

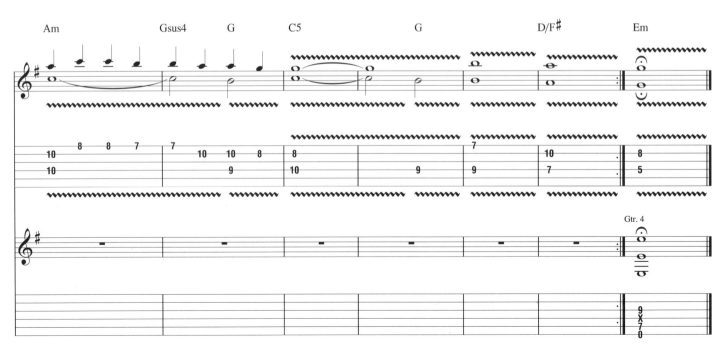

# Everything Will Be Alright

**Words and Music by Brandon Flowers, Dave Keuning, Mark Stoermer and Ronnie Vannucci**

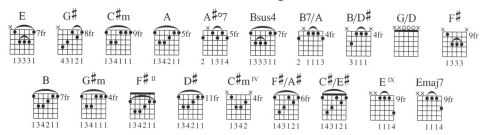

Tune down 1/2 step:
(low to high) Eb-Ab-Db-Gb-Bb-Eb

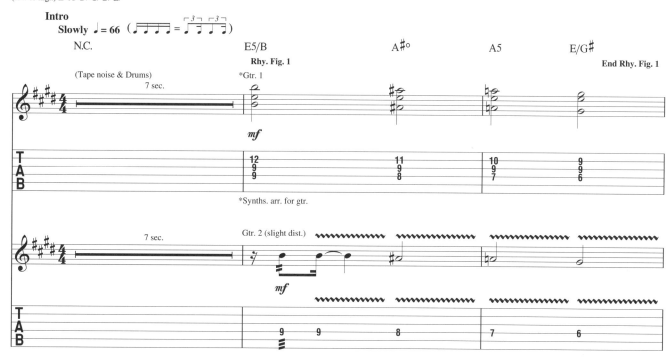

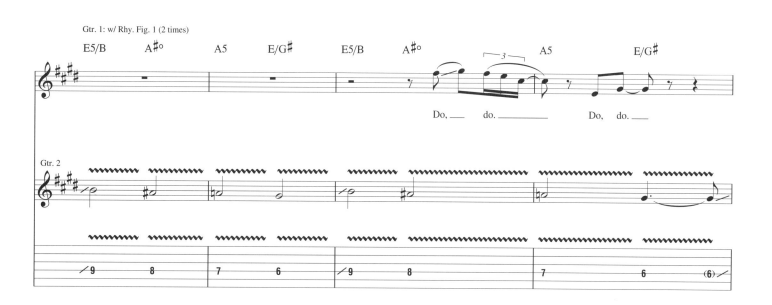

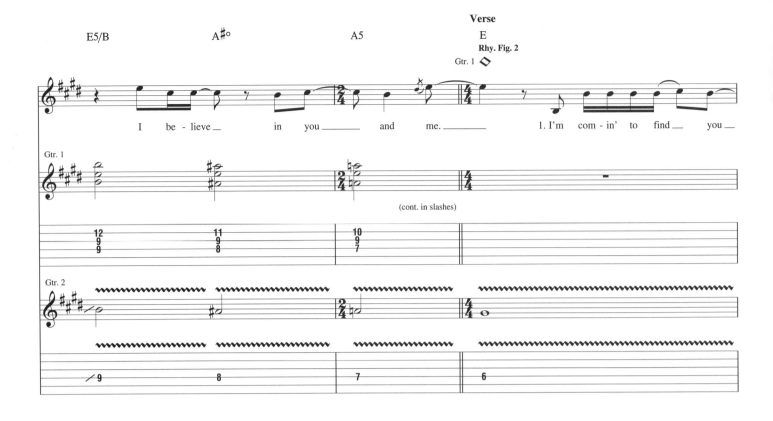

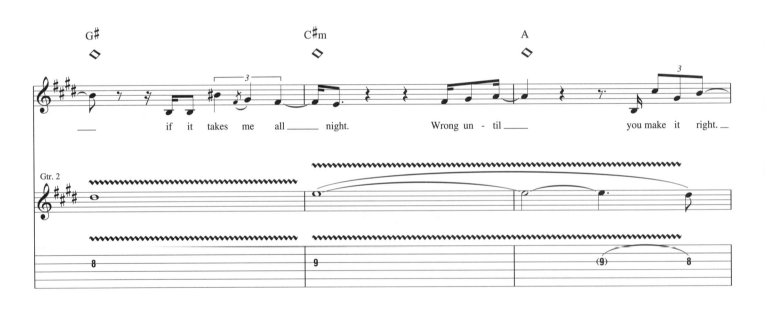

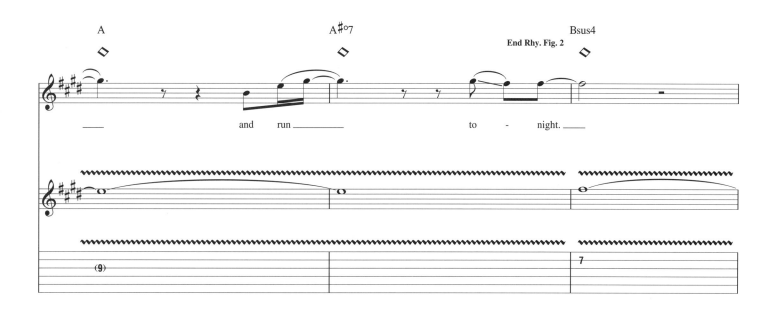

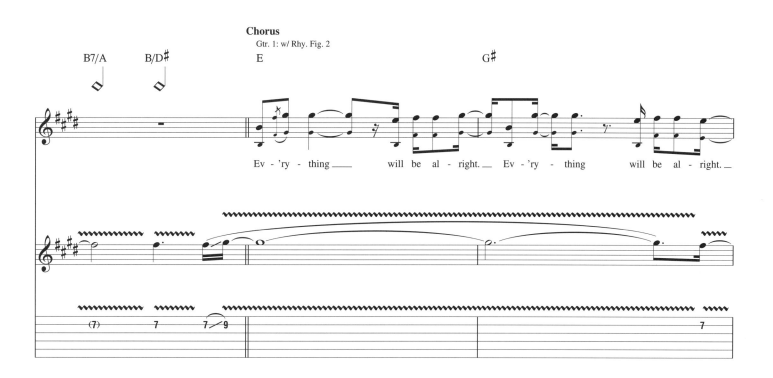

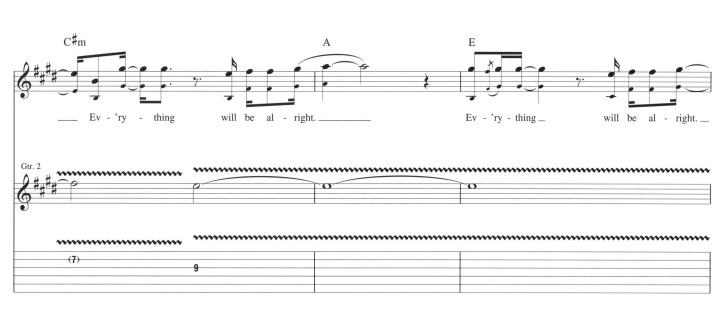

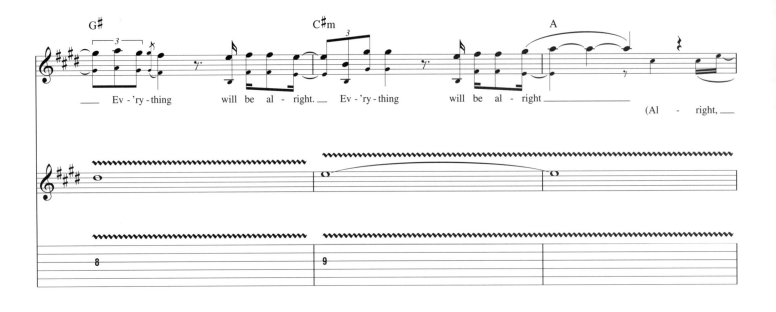

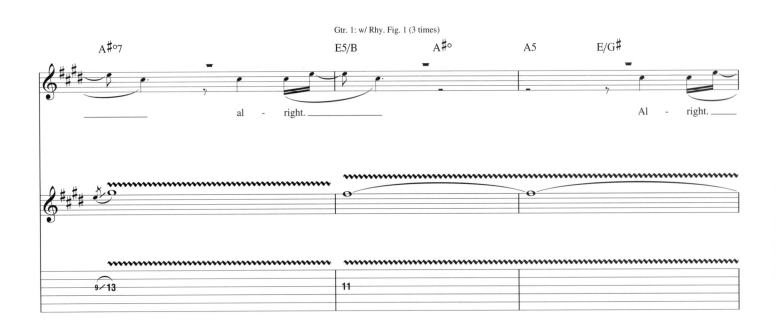

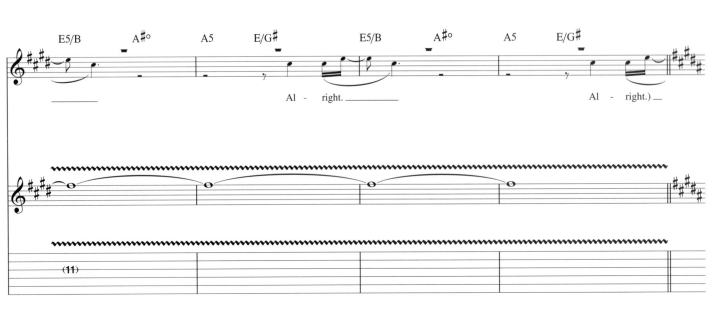

**Verse**

*Synth. arr. for gtr.

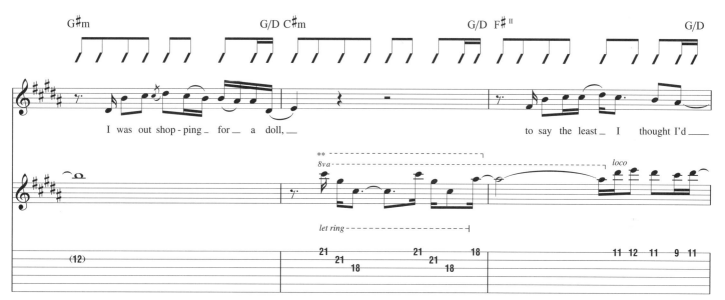

**Played as straight sixteenth-notes.

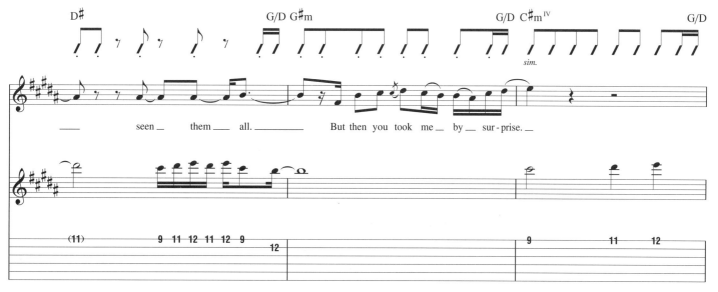

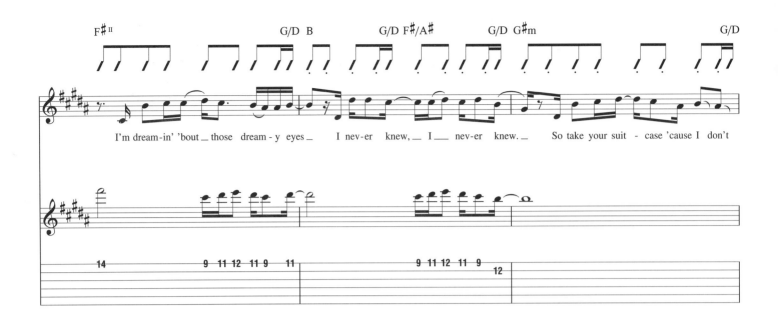

I'm dream-in' 'bout _ those dream - y eyes _ I nev-er knew, _ I _ nev-er knew. _ So take your suit - case 'cause I don't

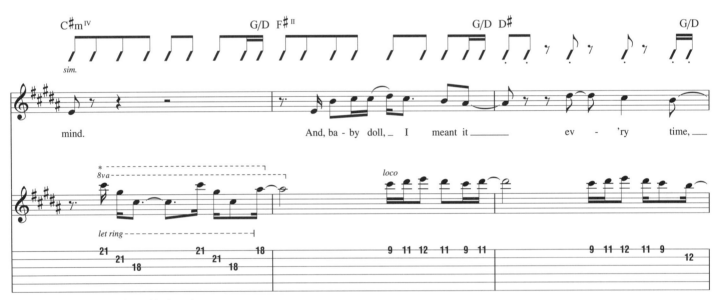

mind.

And, ba - by doll, _ I meant it _____ ev - 'ry time, _

*Played as straight sixteenth-notes.

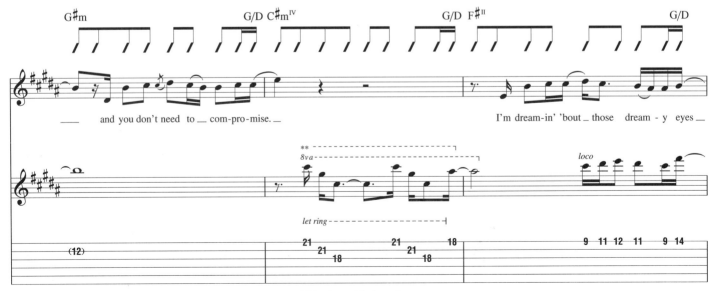

_ and you don't need to _ com-pro-mise. _

I'm dream-in' 'bout _ those dream - y eyes

**Played as straight sixteenth-notes.

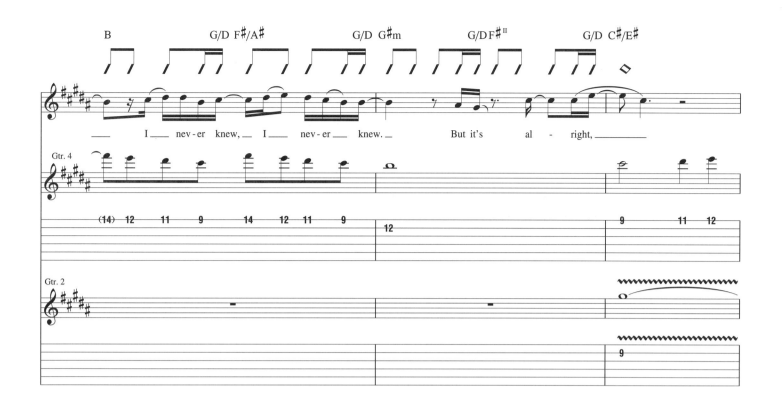

I never knew, I never knew. But it's alright,

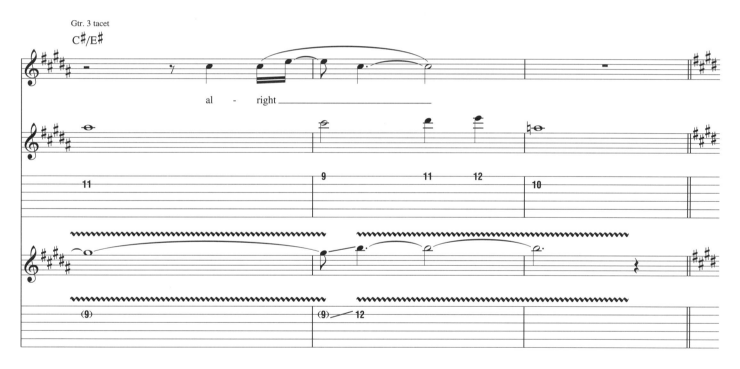

alright

Ev'rything will be alright. Ev'rything will be alright. Ev'rything will be alright.

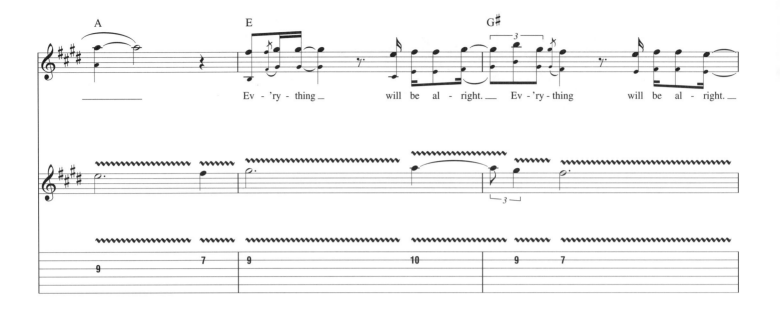

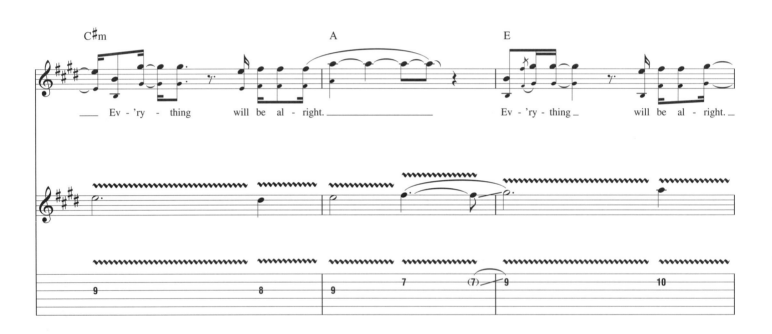

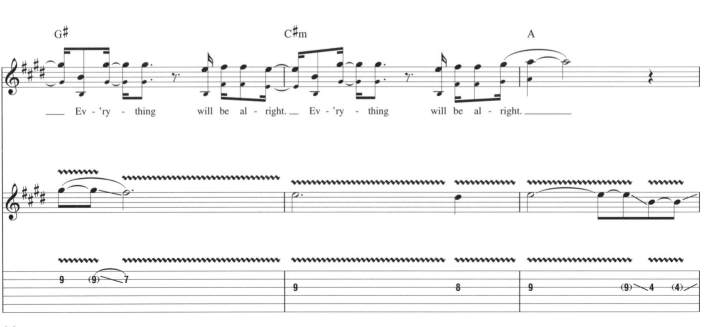

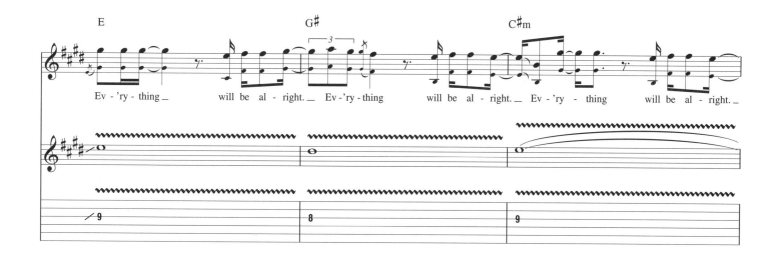

Ev-'ry-thing __ will be al-right. __ Ev-'ry-thing will be al-right. __ Ev-'ry-thing will be al-right. __

**Outro-Guitar Solo**

Gtr. 1: w/ Rhy. Fig. 2 (1st 4 meas.) (3 times)

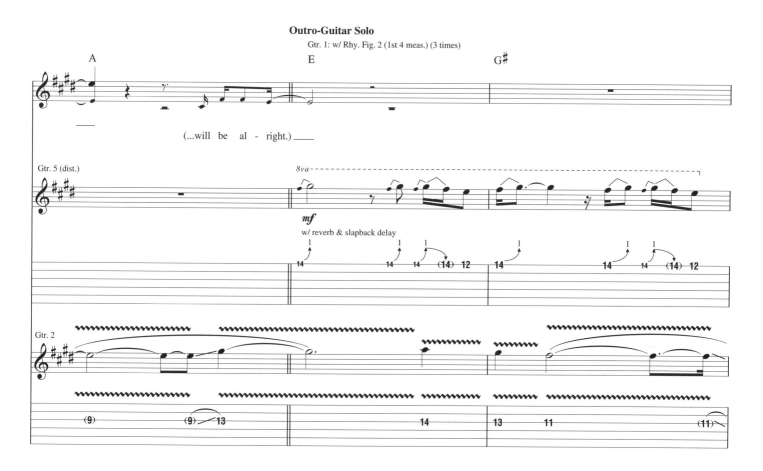

(...will be al - right.) ____

Gtr. 5 (dist.)

*mf*
w/ reverb & slapback delay

Gtr. 2

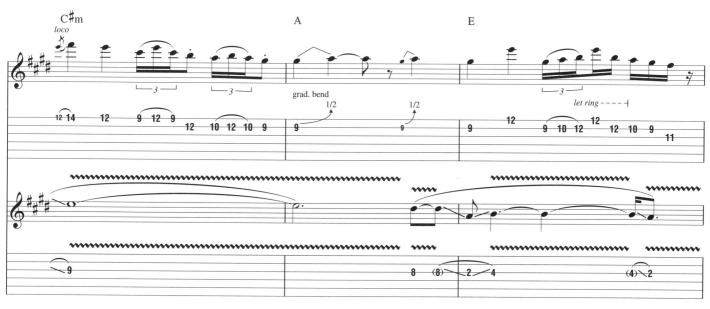

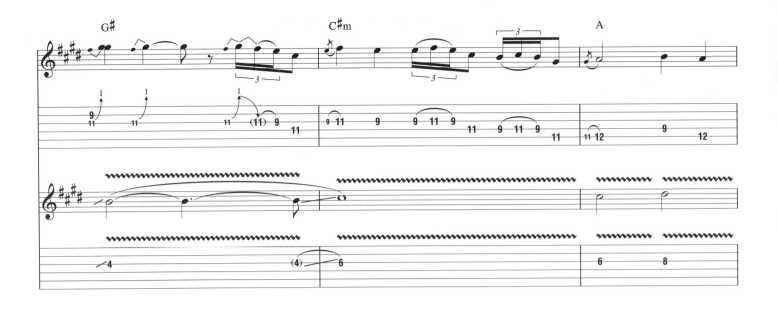

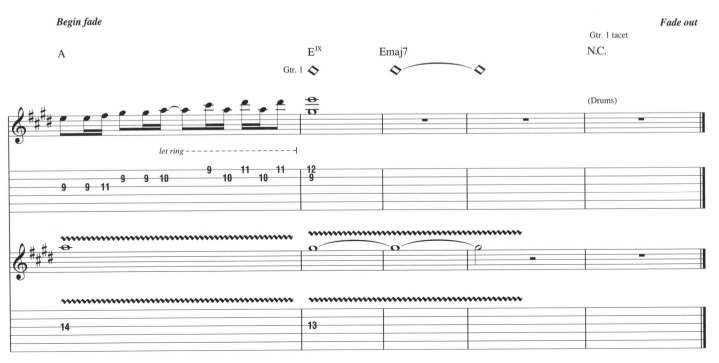

# Guitar Notation Legend

Guitar Music can be notated three different ways: on a *musical staff*, in *tablature*, and in *rhythm slashes*.

**RHYTHM SLASHES** are written above the staff. Strum chords in the rhythm indicated. Use the chord diagrams found at the top of the first page of the transcription for the appropriate chord voicings. Round noteheads indicate single notes.

**THE MUSICAL STAFF** shows pitches and rhythms and is divided by bar lines into measures. Pitches are named after the first seven letters of the alphabet.

**TABLATURE** graphically represents the guitar fingerboard. Each horizontal line represents a string, and each number represents a fret.

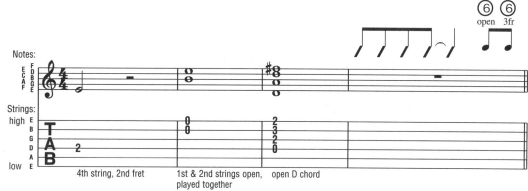

**HALF-STEP BEND:** Strike the note and bend up 1/2 step.

**WHOLE-STEP BEND:** Strike the note and bend up one step.

**GRACE NOTE BEND:** Strike the note and immediately bend up as indicated.

**SLIGHT (MICROTONE) BEND:** Strike the note and bend up 1/4 step.

**BEND AND RELEASE:** Strike the note and bend up as indicated, then release back to the original note. Only the first note is struck.

**PRE-BEND:** Bend the note as indicated, then strike it.

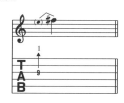

**VIBRATO:** The string is vibrated by rapidly bending and releasing the note with the fretting hand.

**WIDE VIBRATO:** The pitch is varied to a greater degree by vibrating with the fretting hand.

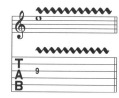

**HAMMER-ON:** Strike the first (lower) note with one finger, then sound the higher note (on the same string) with another finger by fretting it without picking.

**PULL-OFF:** Place both fingers on the notes to be sounded. Strike the first note and without picking, pull the finger off to sound the second (lower) note.

**LEGATO SLIDE:** Strike the first note and then slide the same fret-hand finger up or down to the second note. The second note is not struck.

**SHIFT SLIDE:** Same as legato slide, except the second note is struck.

**TRILL:** Very rapidly alternate between the notes indicated by continuously hammering on and pulling off.

**TAPPING:** Hammer ("tap") the fret indicated with the pick-hand index or middle finger and pull off to the note fretted by the fret hand.

**NATURAL HARMONIC:** Strike the note while the fret-hand lightly touches the string directly over the fret indicated.

**PINCH HARMONIC:** The note is fretted normally and a harmonic is produced by adding the edge of the thumb or the tip of the index finger of the pick hand to the normal pick attack.

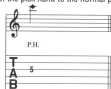

**PICK SCRAPE:** The edge of the pick is rubbed down (or up) the string, producing a scratchy sound.

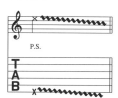

**MUFFLED STRINGS:** A percussive sound is produced by laying the fret hand across the string(s) without depressing, and striking them with the pick hand.

**PALM MUTING:** The note is partially muted by the pick hand lightly touching the string(s) just before the bridge.

**RAKE:** Drag the pick across the strings indicated with a single motion.

**TREMOLO PICKING:** The note is picked as rapidly and continuously as possible.

**VIBRATO BAR DIVE AND RETURN:** The pitch of the note or chord is dropped a specified number of steps (in rhythm) then returned to the original pitch.

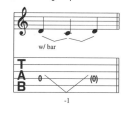

**VIBRATO BAR SCOOP:** Depress the bar just before striking the note, then quickly release the bar.

**VIBRATO BAR DIP:** Strike the note and then immediately drop a specified number of steps, then release back to the original pitch.

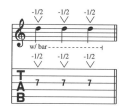

# RECORDED VERSIONS
## *The Best Note-For-Note Transcriptions Available*

**ALL BOOKS INCLUDE TABLATURE**

| | | |
|---|---|---|
| 00690501 Adams, Bryan – Greatest Hits . . . . . . . . . .$19.95 | 00690601 Good Charlotte – | 00690145 Rage Against the Machine – Evil Empire . .$19.95 |
| 00692015 Aerosmith – Greatest Hits . . . . . . . . . . . . .$22.95 | The Young and the Hopeless . . . . . . . . . .$19.95 | 00690426 Ratt – Best of . . . . . . . . . . . . . . . . . . . . . .$19.95 |
| 00690178 Alice in Chains – Acoustic . . . . . . . . . . . . .$19.95 | 00690591 Griffin, Patty – Guitar Collection . . . . . . . .$19.95 | 00690055 Red Hot Chili Peppers – |
| 00690387 Alice in Chains – Nothing Safe: | 00694798 Harrison, George – Anthology . . . . . . . . . .$19.95 | Bloodsugarsexmagik . . . . . . . . . . . . .$19.95 |
| The Best of the Box . . . . . . . . . . . . . . . .$19.95 | 00692930 Hendrix, Jimi – Are You Experienced? . . . .$24.95 | 00690584 Red Hot Chili Peppers – By the Way . . . .$19.95 |
| 00694932 Allman Brothers Band – Volume 1 . . . . . .$24.95 | 00692931 Hendrix, Jimi – Axis: Bold As Love . . . . .$22.95 | 00690379 Red Hot Chili Peppers – Californication . .$19.95 |
| 00694933 Allman Brothers Band – Volume 2 . . . . . .$24.95 | 00690017 Hendrix, Jimi – Live at Woodstock . . . . . .$24.95 | 00690090 Red Hot Chili Peppers – One Hot Minute .$22.95 |
| 00694878 Atkins, Chet – Vintage Fingerstyle . . . . . .$19.95 | 00690602 Hendrix, Jimi – Smash Hits . . . . . . . . . . .$19.95 | 00690511 Reinhardt, Django – Definitive Collection .$19.95 |
| 00690418 Audio Adrenaline, Best of . . . . . . . . . . . .$17.95 | 00660029 Holly, Buddy . . . . . . . . . . . . . . . . . . . . . .$19.95 | 00690643 Relient K – Two Lefts Don't |
| 00690609 Audioslave . . . . . . . . . . . . . . . . . . . . . . . .$19.95 | 00690457 Incubus – Make Yourself . . . . . . . . . . . . . .$19.95 | Make a Right...But Three Do . . . . . . . . . .$19.95 |
| 00690366 Bad Company – Original Anthology, Book 1 . .$19.95 | 00690544 Incubus – Morningview . . . . . . . . . . . . . . .$19.95 | 00690014 Rolling Stones – Exile on Main Street . . . .$24.95 |
| 00690503 Beach Boys – Very Best of . . . . . . . . . . . .$19.95 | 00690136 Indigo Girls – 1200 Curfews . . . . . . . . . . .$22.95 | 00690631 Rolling Stones – Guitar Anthology . . . . . .$24.95 |
| 00690489 Beatles – 1 . . . . . . . . . . . . . . . . . . . . . . . .$24.95 | 00694912 Johnson, Eric – Ah Via Musicom . . . . . . .$19.95 | 00690600 Saliva – Back Into Your System . . . . . . . .$19.95 |
| 00694929 Beatles – 1962-1966 . . . . . . . . . . . . . . . .$24.95 | 00690660 Johnson, Eric – Best of . . . . . . . . . . . . . .$19.95 | 00690031 Santana's Greatest Hits . . . . . . . . . . . . . .$19.95 |
| 00694930 Beatles – 1967-1970 . . . . . . . . . . . . . . . .$24.95 | 00690271 Johnson, Robert – New Transcriptions . . . .$24.95 | 00690566 Scorpions – Best of . . . . . . . . . . . . . . . . .$19.95 |
| 00694832 Beatles – For Acoustic Guitar . . . . . . . . .$19.95 | 00699131 Joplin, Janis – Best of . . . . . . . . . . . . . . .$19.95 | 00690604 Seger, Bob – Guitar Collection . . . . . . . . .$19.95 |
| 00690137 Beatles – A Hard Day's Night . . . . . . . . . .$16.95 | 00690427 Judas Priest – Best of . . . . . . . . . . . . . . .$19.95 | 00690419 Slipknot . . . . . . . . . . . . . . . . . . . . . . . . . .$19.95 |
| 00690482 Beatles – Let It Be . . . . . . . . . . . . . . . . . .$16.95 | 00690504 King, Albert – The Very Best of . . . . . . . . .$19.95 | 00690530 Slipknot – Iowa . . . . . . . . . . . . . . . . . . . .$19.95 |
| 00690632 Beck – Sea Change . . . . . . . . . . . . . . . . . .$19.95 | 00690444 King, B.B. and Eric Clapton – | 00690385 Sonicflood . . . . . . . . . . . . . . . . . . . . . . . .$19.95 |
| 00694884 Benson, George – Best of . . . . . . . . . . . . .$19.95 | Riding with the King . . . . . . . . . . . . . . . .$19.95 | 00690021 Sting – Fields of Gold . . . . . . . . . . . . . . .$19.95 |
| 00692385 Berry, Chuck . . . . . . . . . . . . . . . . . . . . . .$19.95 | 00690339 Kinks, The – Best of . . . . . . . . . . . . . . . .$19.95 | 00690597 Stone Sour . . . . . . . . . . . . . . . . . . . . . . . .$19.95 |
| 00692200 Black Sabbath – | 00690614 Lavigne, Avril – Let Go . . . . . . . . . . . . . .$19.95 | 00690520 Styx Guitar Collection . . . . . . . . . . . . . . .$19.95 |
| We Sold Our Soul for Rock 'N' Roll . . . . .$19.95 | 00690525 Lynch, George – Best of . . . . . . . . . . . . . .$19.95 | 00690519 Sum 41 – All Killer No Filler . . . . . . . . . .$19.95 |
| 00690674 Blink-182 . . . . . . . . . . . . . . . . . . . . . . . . .$19.95 | 00694755 Malmsteen, Yngwie – Rising Force . . . . . .$19.95 | 00690612 Sum 41 – Does This Look Infected? . . . . .$19.95 |
| 00690389 Blink-182 – Enema of the State . . . . . . . . .$19.95 | 00694956 Marley, Bob – Legend . . . . . . . . . . . . . . .$19.95 | 00690425 System of a Down . . . . . . . . . . . . . . . . . .$19.95 |
| 00690523 Blink-182 – Take Off Your Pants & Jacket .$19.95 | 00690548 Marley, Bob – One Love: Very Best of . . .$19.95 | 00690606 System of a Down – Steal This Album . . . .$19.95 |
| 00690028 Blue Oyster Cult – Cult Classics . . . . . . . .$19.95 | 00694945 Marley, Bob – Songs of Freedom . . . . . . .$24.95 | 00690531 System of a Down – Toxicity . . . . . . . . . .$19.95 |
| 00690583 Boxcar Racer . . . . . . . . . . . . . . . . . . . . . .$19.95 | 00690616 Matchbox 20 – More Than You Think You Are .$19.95 | 00694824 Taylor, James – Best of . . . . . . . . . . . . . .$16.95 |
| 00690491 Bowie, David – Best of . . . . . . . . . . . . . . .$19.95 | 00690239 Matchbox 20 – Yourself or Someone Like You .$19.95 | 00690238 Third Eye Blind . . . . . . . . . . . . . . . . . . . .$19.95 |
| 00690451 Buckley, Jeff – Collection . . . . . . . . . . . . .$24.95 | 00690382 McLachlan, Sarah – Mirrorball . . . . . . . . .$19.95 | 00690580 311 – From Chaos . . . . . . . . . . . . . . . . . .$19.95 |
| 00690364 Cake – Songbook . . . . . . . . . . . . . . . . . . .$19.95 | 00694952 Megadeth – Countdown to Extinction . . . .$19.95 | 00690295 Tool – Aenima . . . . . . . . . . . . . . . . . . . . .$19.95 |
| 00690564 Calling, The – Camino Palmero . . . . . . . . .$29.95 | 00694951 Megadeth – Rust in Peace . . . . . . . . . . . .$22.95 | 00690654 Train – Best of . . . . . . . . . . . . . . . . . . . . .$19.95 |
| 00690043 Cheap Trick – Best of . . . . . . . . . . . . . . . .$19.95 | 00690495 Megadeth – The World Needs a Hero . . . .$19.95 | 00690039 Vai, Steve – Alien Love Secrets . . . . . . . . .$24.95 |
| 00690567 Christian, Charlie – Definitive Collection . .$19.95 | 00690505 Mellencamp, John – Guitar Collection . . . .$19.95 | 00690392 Vai, Steve – The Ultra Zone . . . . . . . . . . .$19.95 |
| 00690590 Clapton, Eric – Anthology . . . . . . . . . . . . .$29.95 | 00690562 Metheny, Pat – Bright Size Life . . . . . . . .$19.95 | 00690370 Vaughan, Stevie Ray and Double Trouble – |
| 00692391 Clapton, Eric – Best of, 2nd Edition . . . . .$22.95 | 00690559 Metheny, Pat – Question and Answer . . . . .$19.95 | The Real Deal: Greatest Hits Volume 2 . .$22.95 |
| 00690415 Clapton Chronicles – Best of Eric Clapton .$18.95 | 00690611 Nirvana . . . . . . . . . . . . . . . . . . . . . . . . . .$22.95 | 00690116 Vaughan, Stevie Ray – Guitar Collection . . .$24.95 |
| 00690074 Clapton, Eric – The Cream of Clapton . . . .$24.95 | 00690189 Nirvana – From the Muddy | 00660058 Vaughan, Stevie Ray – |
| 00694869 Clapton, Eric – Unplugged . . . . . . . . . . . .$22.95 | Banks of the Wishkah . . . . . . . . . . . . . . .$19.95 | Lightnin' Blues 1983-1987 . . . . . . . . . . .$24.95 |
| 00690162 Clash, Best of The . . . . . . . . . . . . . . . . . .$19.95 | 00694913 Nirvana – In Utero . . . . . . . . . . . . . . . . . .$19.95 | 00690550 Vaughan, Stevie Ray and Double Trouble – |
| 00690494 Coldplay – Parachutes . . . . . . . . . . . . . . . .$19.95 | 00694883 Nirvana – Nevermind . . . . . . . . . . . . . . . .$19.95 | Live at Montreux 1982 & 1985 . . . . . . . .$24.95 |
| 00690593 Coldplay – A Rush of Blood to the Head . .$19.95 | 00690026 Nirvana – Unplugged in New York . . . . . .$19.95 | 00694835 Vaughan, Stevie Ray – The Sky Is Crying . .$22.95 |
| 00694940 Counting Crows – August & Everything After .$19.95 | 00690121 Oasis – (What's the Story) Morning Glory .$19.95 | 00690015 Vaughan, Stevie Ray – Texas Flood . . . . . .$19.95 |
| 00690401 Creed – Human Clay . . . . . . . . . . . . . . . . .$19.95 | 00690358 Offspring, The – Americana . . . . . . . . . . .$19.95 | 00694789 Waters, Muddy – Deep Blues . . . . . . . . . .$24.95 |
| 00690352 Creed – My Own Prison . . . . . . . . . . . . . . .$19.95 | 00690485 Offspring, The – Conspiracy of One . . . . .$19.95 | 00690071 Weezer (The Blue Album) . . . . . . . . . . . .$19.95 |
| 00690551 Creed – Weathered . . . . . . . . . . . . . . . . . .$19.95 | 00690552 Offspring, The – Ignition . . . . . . . . . . . . .$19.95 | 00690516 Weezer (The Green Album) . . . . . . . . . . .$19.95 |
| 00699521 Cure, The – Greatest Hits . . . . . . . . . . . . .$24.95 | 00690663 Offspring, The – Splinter . . . . . . . . . . . . .$19.95 | 00690579 Weezer – Maladroit . . . . . . . . . . . . . . . . .$19.95 |
| 00690484 dc Talk – Intermission: The Greatest Hits .$19.95 | 00694847 Osbourne, Ozzy – Best of . . . . . . . . . . . .$22.95 | 00690286 Weezer – Pinkerton . . . . . . . . . . . . . . . . .$19.95 |
| 00690289 Deep Purple, Best of . . . . . . . . . . . . . . . .$17.95 | 00690547 Osbourne, Ozzy – Down to Earth . . . . . . .$19.95 | 00690447 Who, The – Best of . . . . . . . . . . . . . . . . .$24.95 |
| 00690563 Default – The Fallout . . . . . . . . . . . . . . . .$19.95 | 00690399 Osbourne, Ozzy – Ozzman Cometh . . . . . .$19.95 | 00690640 Wilcox, David – Anthology 2000-2003 . . .$19.95 |
| 00690384 Di Franco, Ani – Best of . . . . . . . . . . . . . .$19.95 | 00694855 Pearl Jam – Ten . . . . . . . . . . . . . . . . . . . .$19.95 | 00690320 Williams, Dar – Best of . . . . . . . . . . . . . .$17.95 |
| 00695382 Dire Straits – Sultans of Swing . . . . . . . . .$19.95 | 00690439 Perfect Circle, A – Mer De Noms . . . . . . .$19.95 | 00690596 Yardbirds, The – Best of . . . . . . . . . . . . .$19.95 |
| 00690347 Doors, The – Anthology . . . . . . . . . . . . . .$22.95 | 00690499 Petty, Tom – The Definitive | 00690443 Zappa, Frank – Hot Rats . . . . . . . . . . . . .$19.95 |
| 00690348 Doors, The – Essential Guitar Collection . .$16.95 | Guitar Collection . . . . . . . . . . . . . . . . . .$19.95 | 00690589 ZZ Top Guitar Anthology . . . . . . . . . . . . .$22.95 |
| 00690555 Etheridge, Melissa – Best of . . . . . . . . . . .$19.95 | 00690424 Phish – Farmhouse . . . . . . . . . . . . . . . . .$19.95 | |
| 00690524 Etheridge, Melissa – Skin . . . . . . . . . . . . .$19.95 | 00690240 Phish – Hoist . . . . . . . . . . . . . . . . . . . . . .$19.95 | |
| 00690515 Extreme II – Pornograffitti . . . . . . . . . . . .$19.95 | 00690607 Phish – Round Room . . . . . . . . . . . . . . . .$19.95 | |
| 00690235 Foo Fighters – The Colour and the Shape .$19.95 | 00690331 Phish – Story of the Ghost . . . . . . . . . . . .$19.95 | |
| 00690595 Foo Fighters – One by One . . . . . . . . . . . .$19.95 | 00690642 Pillar – Fireproof . . . . . . . . . . . . . . . . . . .$19.95 | |
| 00690394 Foo Fighters – | 00690428 Pink Floyd – Dark Side of the Moon . . . . .$19.95 | |
| There Is Nothing Left to Lose . . . . . . . . .$19.95 | 00690546 P.O.D. – Satellite . . . . . . . . . . . . . . . . . . .$19.95 | |
| 00690222 G3 Live – Satriani, Vai, Johnson . . . . . . .$22.95 | 00693864 Police, The – Best of . . . . . . . . . . . . . . . .$19.95 | |
| 00690338 Goo Goo Dolls – Dizzy Up the Girl . . . . . .$19.95 | 00690299 Presley, Elvis – Best of Elvis: | |
| 00690576 Goo Goo Dolls – Gutterflower . . . . . . . . .$19.95 | The King of Rock 'n' Roll . . . . . . . . . . . .$19.95 | |
| | 00694975 Queen – Greatest Hits . . . . . . . . . . . . . . .$24.95 | |
| | 00694910 Rage Against the Machine . . . . . . . . . . . .$19.95 | |